# Asperger's—
# If You Only Knew

# Asperger's—
# If You Only Knew

## "A Family's Struggle with Asperger's Syndrome"

*Sophia Summers*

iUniverse, Inc.
New York Lincoln Shanghai

Asperger's—If You Only Knew
"A Family's Struggle with Asperger's Syndrome"

iUniverse books may be ordered through booksellers or by contacting:

iUniverse
2021 Pine Lake Road, Suite 100
Lincoln, NE 68512
www.iuniverse.com
1-800-Authors (1-800-288-4677)

ISBN: 978-0-595-44932-3 (pbk)
ISBN: 978-0-595-89254-9 (ebk)

Printed in the United States of America

*This book is my legacy to you, my son. I hope it will help you appreciate and understand yourself for the wonderful person that you are. My wish for you is that you realize your true potential through the unique intellectual capacities of the Asperger mind. You constantly amaze me.*

# Contents

# Introduction

# An Inside Perspective of the Asperger Mind

Ever since the words "autism" and "Asperger's syndrome" made their way into our lives, I have come across various descriptions of these syndromes. At the time, there were limited resources for Asperger's syndrome, and the closest material I could find was on high-functioning autism.

Since my son Josh's diagnosis of Asperger's syndrome, I've spent many years scouring books, articles, and the Internet for information, hoping to find peace of mind through stories closely depicting our situation. Some of the best Web sites and books on autism spectrum disorders can be accessed in the suggested reading section of this book. The combination of this information with my own personal experience has helped me locate some of the missing pieces Josh and I needed in order to lead rewarding lives. Although I didn't recognize it in myself until recently, I feel fortunate that I was able to see and appreciate AS from both perspectives.

My name is Sophia Summers. I live in the greater Toronto area with my husband and our two children. My professional background includes a college education and a career in sales and marketing. However, Asperger's syndrome has been my personal field of study for most of my adult life. My son and I both fit on the high-functioning spectrum. As children, our symptoms were more prominent. Through various coping methods and learned social skills, our symptoms have somewhat diminished. I wrote this book so that parents, professionals, and people on the spectrum could better understand the true core of autism spectrum disorders. A book written by someone as high-functioning as we are would have given me and my family a source of comfort, hope, and direction. That being said, I am inviting you into our lives in the hopes that I can bring you a bit of the comfort I so sorely needed.

As a child, it was understood that there was something different about me, but the doctor couldn't explain it, which was all the more frustrating for my parents. It was difficult to pinpoint, since the main areas of my development seemed to be on target. They understood, however, that my tendency to go into daydream mode, not to mention my forgetfulness, was beyond my control. They knew I had difficulties expressing myself, but no one had the answers. I can't imagine how discouraging that must have been for them throughout the years. As an adult, my condition is considered mild, and one of my most positive Asperger traits is an obsession with reading and writing. Writing helps me to better organize my thoughts, and I find it therapeutic. This, combined with raising a child with Asperger's syndrome, allows me to give you a unique perspective into both worlds.

Josh is very much like every other kid his age. He has a caring personality and is extremely intelligent. He's often mistakenly seen as being shy and independent. He has a logical point of view, a unique sense of humor, and a tendency to get absorbed in certain interests like computers, bass guitar, art, and cats. He has strong opinions on politics and despises any form of gossip. Watching him grow into adulthood has shown me that the two of us are more alike than I ever imagined. All the stages in Josh's life reminded me of my own childhood. Because we share this common bond, Josh was always able to open up to me with his emotions. I have always been able to connect to him. I instinctively knew exactly what he needed because I recognized the anxiety I saw in him.

We both share an amazing gift for recall. Our long-term memories are remarkable, but we both have terrible short-term memories. Surprisingly, the ability to remember things in vivid detail is somewhat of a curse, because it's difficult to let go of the emotions associated with the memories. I often find myself instantly transferred into the sights and sounds of the past. It is truly a blessing to be able to refer to past experiences with accuracy, and I am able to use this gift in a multitude of situations, like this book.

If you were to meet Josh and me, you wouldn't know we have Asperger's syndrome. Not unless you spent enough time with us and you were able to recognize the symptoms. For both of us, the external symptoms are so minute it's often difficult to pinpoint them. Josh is gifted in all areas involving computers, and I have a driving need to read and write. To me, a book is like a security blanket. It's an escape into my own world.

However, if you were to step into our shoes, you would find that the internal symptoms can be quite intense. These strong gifts and desires would consume your thoughts. For example, you'd feel most comfortable frequenting the same places and sitting at the same table. On the other hand, if you found yourself in a familiar but crowded place, you might want to participate, but you would most likely prefer to be alone. The confusing buzz of conversation would drive you to retreat into your own fantasy world, blocking out all your surroundings. If something captured your interest and you wanted to express yourself, you would know exactly what to say but wouldn't know quite how to begin or continue. Once you'd mustered the courage to start to say it and the words came out all wrong, your anxieties would take over.

On the other hand, if you were to find yourself in a state of anxiety in a crowded, unfamiliar place, you might be consumed with a vulnerability you couldn't explain. You would also be consumed with a feeling of awkwardness and a constant awareness of being exposed or disconnected (professionals refer to this as a feeling of displacement). At times, you'd wonder if anyone noticed how you were walking and if your posture was right. That's right—for some reason, it's difficult to maintain good posture. You'd try not to get caught making the faint, rhythmic motions you subconsciously make in order to feel grounded, such as finger tapping or blinking when you're deep in thought. This tends to happen more in times of anxiety. Josh tends to walk in a repetitive pattern, especially if he's explaining something. He says it helps him focus on what he's saying and gives him something to do. Throughout all of this, you'd wonder, or rather envy, how everyone else can seemingly go about their days oblivious and comfortable in their surroundings.

Driving and carrying on a conversation can be difficult for me, and my sense of direction is awful. Anyone who knows me understands that if they talk to me, I'll miss the turn and I'll have to backtrack again.

Because of these difficulties, I have been a student of human nature in search of normality for as long as I can remember. Because of my difficulties in life, I tend to gravitate to psychology or self-help books.

Many people now refer to Asperger's syndrome in its short form, AS. I prefer this because it omits the word "syndrome." If there is something to be thankful for, it's that AS is by far one of the most fascinating conditions in the history of mental health. Some of the most gifted individuals in history were thought to have had AS: Albert Einstein, Thomas Jefferson, and Michelangelo, just to name a few. Today, some of the most brilliant people are thought to share these traits, like Bill Gates, the Microsoft guru, and Steven Spielberg, the famous movie producer. I have to say that this alone is probably one of the most encouraging pieces of information for those facing this disorder, as it offers much hope for the individual's future. That being said, the downside is that AS, or autism, can be quite debilitating if it's not properly understood or dealt with. This is often the case with someone who goes undiagnosed, which is all too common.

My inspiration to write this book was born from a dream I had of Josh discovering my death. My dreams are very graphic, much like a movie in all the details and emotions. Dreaming is a source of entertainment for me, and I still look forward to sleeping for that reason. In the dream, Josh had amnesia, and he was suddenly remembering details of my death with horrible anguish and desperation. He was talking to me, but I was someone else (his guardian, I'm guessing). I was trying to comfort him, but I couldn't reach him. He was looking through me, and I felt totally helpless.

This dream seemed very real. I woke up in tears and couldn't get the dream out of my mind. It took over two years for me to realize that the woman I was in that dream was not my true self. That's why I couldn't comfort him.

> Was it possible that he was mourning the mother that I was hiding deep inside? I couldn't help thinking that maybe he simply needed me to accept him for who he was. Then it occurred to me that the only way I could do that was to accept myself.

This book depicts the struggles my son and I faced growing up with AS, the eventual diagnosis I sought for myself, as well as our battle to overcome and embrace the intriguing qualities associated with this syndrome. Out of respect for my loved ones, I have used fictional names to give you an accurate account of my experiences without reservations. The events in this book are exact accounts of the challenges and experiences of living with AS from both perspectives. This book delves deeply into the most personal and brutally honest aspects of my thoughts, and Josh's as well, of the challenges we face on a daily basis. You will get a firsthand account of how it has affected us individually and the coping methods we use in our daily lives. Most importantly, I will bring you into the role of parenting a child with AS and explain how I used my own experiences to help my son through the difficult times. I will take you through the obsessions that surfaced throughout our journeys, along with the motivations behind our thought processes. As you read through the book, you will see that the coping mechanisms I used for myself and Josh appear in text boxes. This will give you a unique perspective, as well as a better understanding of how to handle the difficulties associated with autism spectrum disorders.

The logic or reasoning behind the actions of someone with AS is often a mystery. You will be surprised to learn that what is perceived on the surface doesn't necessarily represent its true meaning. Perception has many faces, and what you see on the outside is far from what goes on inside the AS mind. By understanding this perspective, I am certain you will make great strides in your own lives and the lives of your loved ones.

One of my main goals is to be able to reach the many people harboring uncertainties about their existence. I hope I can provide some answers and important coping skills.

*Writing this book has helped me rediscover the mysteries of how and why I've always related to my world. It has forced me to muster the courage to show others my true self and to realize that I was my worst critic. Putting it all into words has helped me understand and forgive myself for things I couldn't control, and to embrace the unique qualities that come with AS.*

# Chapter 1

# Asperger's Epidemic Proportions

According to the National Center on Birth Defects and Developmental Disabilities, it is estimated that approximately one in 150 children are diagnosed with an autism spectrum disorder (ASD). ASDs are known to be more common amongst boys than girls. This figure has risen dramatically from three in ten thousand in the early nineties. This study doesn't include adults or the undiagnosed population. Many believe we're in the middle of an epidemic. Others say the increase is due to better awareness and proper diagnosis. Whatever it is, we need to find ideal solutions, and fast. Although there is much controversy surrounding the differences between autism and Asperger's syndrome, it is now known that Asperger's and high-functioning autism share the same characteristics. Asperger's, though, is characterized by an average, above-average, or exceptionally high IQ; while low-functioning autism is characterized by a speech deficiency before the age of three, combined with a below-average IQ. Asperger's is considered more recently to be the bridge from neuro-typical (the term used for normal) to high-functioning autism.

I have compiled a wealth of information from The National Institute of Neurological Disorders and Stroke National Institutes of Health Bethesda, MD 20892. Their research indicates that Asperger Syndrome (AS) is an autism spectrum disorder (ASD), one of a distinct group of neurological conditions characterized by a greater or lesser degree of impairment in language and communication skills, as well as repetitive or restrictive patterns of thought and behavior. Other ASDs include: classic autism, Rett syndrome, childhood disintegrative disorder, and pervasive developmental disorder not otherwise specified (usually referred to as PDD-NOS).

Parents usually sense there is something unusual about a child with AS by the time of his or her third birthday, and some children may exhibit symptoms as early as infancy. Unlike children with autism, children with AS retain their early language skills. Motor development delays—crawling or walking late, clumsiness—are sometimes the first indicator of the disorder.

Studies of children with AS suggest that their problems with socialization and communication continue into adulthood. Some of these children develop additional psychiatric symptoms and disorders in adolescence and adulthood.

Although diagnosed mainly in children, AS is being increasingly diagnosed in adults who seek medical help for mental health conditions such as depression, obsessive-compulsive disorder (OCD), and attention deficit hyperactivity disorder (ADHD). No studies have yet been conducted to determine the incidence of AS in adult populations.

The most distinguishing symptom of AS is a child's obsessive interest in a single object or topic to the exclusion of any other. Some children with AS have become experts on vacuum cleaners, makes and models of cars, even objects as odd as deep fat fryers. Children with AS want to know everything about their topic of interest and their conversations with others will be about little else. Their expertise, high level of vocabulary, and formal speech patterns make them seem like little professors. Children with AS will gather enormous amounts of factual information about their favorite subject and will talk incessantly about it, but the conversation may seem like a random collection of facts or statistics, with no point or conclusion. Their speech may be marked by a lack of rhythm, an odd inflection, or a monotone pitch. Children with AS often lack the ability to modulate the volume of their voice to match their surroundings. For example, they will have to be reminded to talk softly every time they enter a library or a movie theatre.

Unlike the severe withdrawal from the rest of the world that is characteristic of autism, children with AS are isolated because of their poor social skills and narrow interests. In fact, they may approach other people, but make normal conversation impossible by inappropriate or eccentric behavior, or by wanting only to talk about their singular interest. Children with AS usually have a history of developmental delays in motor skills such as pedaling a bike, catching a ball, or climbing outdoor play equipment. They are often awkward and poorly coordinated with a walk that can appear either stilted or bouncy.

Many children with AS are highly active in early childhood, and then develop anxiety or depression in young adulthood. Other conditions that often co-exist with AS are ADHD, tic disorders (such as Tourette syndrome), depression, anxiety disorders, and OCD.

Current research points to brain abnormalities as the cause of AS. Using advanced brain imaging techniques, scientists have revealed structural and functional differences in specific regions of the brains of normal versus AS children. These defects are most likely caused by the abnormal migration of embryonic cells during fetal development that affects brain structure and "wiring" and then goes on to affect the neural circuits that control thought and behavior.

For example, one study found a reduction of brain activity in the frontal lobe of AS children when they were asked to respond to tasks that required them to use their judgment. Another study found differences in activity when children were asked to respond to facial expressions. A different study investigating brain function in adults with AS revealed abnormal levels of specific proteins that correlate with obsessive and repetitive behaviors.

Scientists have always known that there had to be a genetic component to AS and the other ASDs because of their tendency to run in families. Additional evidence for the link between inherited genetic mutations and AS was observed in the higher incidence of family members who have behavioral symptoms similar to AS but in a more limited form. For example, they had slight difficulties with social interaction, language, or reading.

A specific gene for AS, however, has never been identified. Instead, the most recent research indicates that there are most likely a common group of genes whose variations or deletions make an individual vulnerable to developing AS. This combination of genetic variations or deletions will determine the severity and symptoms for each individual with AS.

With effective treatment, children with AS can learn to cope with their disabilities, but they may still find social situations and personal relationships challenging. Many adults with AS are able to work successfully in mainstream jobs, although they may continue to need encouragement and moral support to maintain an independent life.

Recently, a team of brain scientists at Carnegie Mellon University and the University of Pittsburgh made a startling discovery involving a deficiency in the coordination between the brain's two main language areas. This theory offers hope by suggesting that a cognitive behavioral therapy might be developed in the near future to stimulate the brain's connectivity in these areas.

Because ASDs are spectrum disorders there are no two people completely alike. They can experience different symptoms and severity of symptoms. There are no specific treatments. There is no cure. Social skills training, educational interventions, psychotherapy, and medication have been found to be effective. Desensitizing techniques have also been known to help build coping skills.

There seems to be somewhat of a strain of AS in our family. Out of respect for them, I have to generalize in this situation. Many of the major characteristics associated with AS can be observed in as many as half a dozen of my relatives, some of whom have already passed away. They are known to be extremely focused, but forgetful. Some consider them to be workaholics or driven types, and they are all very intelligent. They share the same personality traits: they are quirky, yet honorable, kind-hearted individuals with a strong, silent demeanor. Above all, they embrace their solitude. I always felt a strong connection to those individuals. I think the genetic factor can make Asperger's difficult to detect, due to the fact that those who grow up with it consider it merely to be personality traits that the family shares.

Two of my uncles, both of whom were thought to have autistic traits, suffered tremendously, and one committed suicide as a young man. It is vital for me to stress that the after effects of suicide are undeniably some of the most horrific, life-changing tragedies any loved ones could ever deal with. Suicide's intensity overshadows the many fond memories they could have had about that person. Parents, siblings, children, and extended family and friends are plagued with heartrending helplessness, unanswered questions, and doubts, lasting anywhere from a year to an entire lifetime. In the case of our uncle, his loss was so devastating that his name was rarely mentioned after his death.

In many instances, especially into adulthood, many people go through life undiagnosed and plagued with questions about why they feel so odd in comparison to others. In essence, they may share the family traits called AS, but they will rarely admit their raw emotions to each other. Therefore, they remain alone in limbo with their feelings of inadequacy.

If relatives had similar characteristics when younger, they have a unique advantage in helping the child. They know what the child is going through.

This rings true even if the relative is unaware that he or she has this condition. They have the capability and the instincts to identify with the child through their own experiences, and they can offer their guidance.

# Chapter 2

# Earliest Childhood
# Thoughts and Memories

I would like to start out by describing the features and emotions I had as a child in order to give you a thorough understanding of what goes on inside the mind of a child with AS. You will get a firsthand look at the different stages of my life from childhood to adulthood, along with my struggles and coping strategies.

The very first memory I can recall as a toddler was sitting up in my crib. My mother was walking into my bedroom. My mother, Noëlyne, is a sweet and delicate woman, yet she's strong. She would tear anyone apart if it meant protecting her kids or husband. I can still visualize it like it happened yesterday, along with my surroundings and emotions in that moment. I would have been about two and a half years old at the most (as verified by my mother), and I knew it was morning by the way the sunlight shone across the room. I remember my mother opening the door to peek in. My first thought, even without words, was, *Oh*! I was startled. Then she chuckled and closed the door. There were no words yet; I couldn't verbalize my thoughts, but the feelings were there. I began talking shortly afterward, and it was quite some time before I was able to dress myself in the morning.

My parents often commented that I was a good baby, and I was content to keep myself busy. As a child, I loved spinning around in circles in our living room and then watching the crown molding on the ceiling distort. The tingling sensation that washed over my body and mind from being dizzy was addictive. I also remember sitting on my bed and blasting out loud, sharp screams because I enjoyed the tickling vibrations it gave me at the top of my skull. It was a liberating experience to me, and it especially amazed me that I could tickle my brain without using my hands. I was also known for reorganizing my bedroom furniture as early as four years old. It took me forever, but the sequence made sense to me and gave me a sense of satisfaction.

My dad, Jacques, is a strong, dependable, serious man with a tenderness that could comfort without words. I thought he was the best-looking man around, and I admired him. Each morning, I systematically watched out my bedroom window where I could only see part of the garage door. As soon as it slammed shut and I knew he was gone, I'd sneak to the kitchen table, gulp down the rest of his coffee, and climb back into bed.

I didn't seem to notice those around me. I grew up with three older brothers and a sister three years younger. I mostly kept to myself, doing my own thing. Every so often, something captured my attention and I'd notice them around me. It was a lot like arriving at an event right in the middle of it, with no beginning or end. It was somewhat confusing. At times I enjoyed the moment, but it wasn't long before I was by myself again, with my own thoughts.

When I went outside to play, I stayed in the yard like I was supposed to, never passing our driveway, where I either stood or walked back and forth listening to the sparrows sing. To me, they were the most beautiful sounds on the face of the earth, and they filled me with joy. To this day, when I hear a sparrow chirping in the spring, it brings me right back to that day, and I can still feel the same familiar joy.

I've always been intrigued with shapes, like stones, for instance. I lined them up from biggest to smallest, admiring their shapes and colors. I still notice shapes in stains on pavement, and I have a fascination with heart-shaped accidental stains. It seems I could spot details quite easily due to my ability to focus on parts of things, rather than seeing everything in a panoramic view. Most of all, I believe it has something to do with my tendency to look down while walking, which I believe is also associated with AS.

# Chapter 3

## Perceptions and Intellectual Awakenings

I was three years old when my parents gave me a notebook to practice writing letters and numbers. I practiced each day and it was at that age that I realized how much I loved to learn.

The older I got, the longer I could pay attention, especially if something interested me.

They began teaching me how to read and write. From this moment on, I saw my parents through different eyes. I was motivated to pay closer attention to what they were saying because I wanted to learn about everything. If I thought I missed something good, I asked them to repeat it. My father was great for that. He would patiently correct me until I got it right. I was so intrigued with the written word. My father prided himself on teaching me the proper manners a little girl should have, and I will always cherish the time he spent doing so. Without even realizing it, he gave me the proper coping skills to deal with social situations. He taught me to say please and thank you. He taught me the importance of looking at the person addressing me as much as possible, waiting for a gap in a conversation to speak and explained it was a sign of respect.

If I forgot, he just had to give me his private look, and that was my cue to check my behavior. I wonder if he worked so diligently with me because of the many times that I embarrassed him or if he felt I needed extra attention in order to prepare me for life. Could it be that he recognized my zest for learning and happily taught me all he could? My father had so much expression on his face that it was difficult to make out his mood. Most times it was difficult to tell what his expression meant, so I would ask him if the crack in his forehead meant that he was mad or that he was going to laugh. I eventually caught on to the basics and learned all the rote behaviors and was quick to assume the proper role expected of me. Appropriate behavior was of the utmost importance to him. Every day for me was a learning experience, and I was able to go through the proper motions as long as there were no surprises.

For instance, when I was four, my uncle Jacob came to visit. He was nothing like my other uncles, who were sturdy and strong like my dad. He looked old and frail and was around five feet tall, and he wore glasses. He was trying to talk to me during this visit, when I asked him to take off his glasses. He did, and I was absolutely horrified at his deep-set eyes surrounded by dark circles and wrinkled skin, and without thinking, I exclaimed, "Oh! You look like a monster!" My father patiently corrected me, saying that what I said wasn't polite and told his brother I didn't know what that word meant. I respected my father, but I tried to argue that it was true and that I knew what that word meant. I found it strange and frustrating that he made excuses for me. He did his best to correct my "habits" as he called them, such as blinking a lot and wringing my hands. All he had to do was give me *the look*, which reminded me to be aware of what I was doing.

My mother commented on the adorable way I tilted my head slightly when I listened to something. She seemed to find most of my features endearing. She always knew how to comfort me and make me feel secure. My mother and I shared an unspoken bond, and I was glad that she gave me the freedom I needed to enjoy my daydreams of replaying television shows or riding a horse. She rarely interrupted me, because she knew it was difficult to get my attention without upsetting me. Unfortunately, she was often depressed or anxious and spent time worrying about many things. As a matter of fact, my mother was hospitalized for depression throughout our childhood. It happened each year for about ten years, and it seemed to affect my siblings more than it did me. That's probably because I had a way to escape into my own world. In hindsight, my parents weren't perfect, but they complemented each other. They overcame the odds and gave us an abundance of love and understanding.

# Chapter 4

# Night Terrors

My parents often played cards in the kitchen with my aunts and uncles. I was sitting alone in the living room, wearing a new pair of pajamas. There were little, striped men on them, and when I moved, it looked like they were moving, too. I sat on the living room chair whimpering and unable to move. It occurred to me to scream for help, but then I realized that the little men on my pajamas might just run all over me. I just sat alone in the living room, terrified and on the verge of tears, until my mother noticed me. Needless to say, I never wore those or any other pajamas again (until I was in my teens).

On a regular basis, I had night terrors about being completely covered in spiders. The dreams were so real that I felt them biting me, and I swear the bites stung even after I awoke. My dream state was and still is very realistic, full of vivid sights and sounds, much like a detailed movie. I quickly developed arachnophobia, which lasted for over eight years. Most kids dread bedtime because their day is ending; I dreaded the inescapable torture I was about to relive each and every night.

It was a Saturday afternoon when I watched my first documentary. I was only four, but as soon as I heard the word "dream," I was all ears. As I watched and listened carefully in hopes of finding an answer to my problems, I was unprepared for what I heard next. The scientist explained that everyone dreams every night and that people must dream, otherwise they would die. As I watched, I felt sheer panic rising in my chest. I desperately asked my brother Rick if that was true, and he said, "Yes, we all have to dream to live." I didn't know the difference between dreams or nightmares and started to cry uncontrollably. I didn't want to dream anymore. The despair I felt at that very moment was unbelievable. I couldn't think of anything else except the fact that I would have to relive the same nightmare night after night with no relief in sight.

He managed to calm me down and said most people have good dreams. "You will, too. All you have to do is think about something you really like, and you will probably dream about it."

Rick gave me my first real coping skill. I thought of Bugs Bunny as I lay in bed and replayed my favorite episodes. It worked some of the time; however, I still had nightmares quite regularly and woke up screaming. It angered me to know that others didn't have to endure the nightmares I did, and I looked forward to the day that I would grow into normalcy. This wasn't normal; I knew that. And nothing could protect me from my mind, not even myself.

Eventually, I became very good at using my new skill. At times, I was able to control my dreams by thinking about something pleasant until I fell asleep.

The day we picked up my baby sister at the hospital, there was a huge fuss. My mom was sitting in the front seat with the baby. I stood leaning over the backseat and looked over to find my baby sister, Natalie, in my mother's arms. Her eyes were a piercing black and her skin was so fair. I remember my mother commenting how the baby looked just like a little mouse. I took it literally, had a second look, and thought to myself, *That's not right. She looks like a baby, not a mouse.* I didn't feel jealousy or excitement and only briefly noticed my brothers and father were with us as well.

When we arrived, my mother placed her on her bed. We weren't usually allowed in our parents' bedroom, and I was confused and reluctant about going in to see her. To me, rules were comforting and predictable. I knew where I stood and basically didn't like exceptions. I reluctantly went in to see her, but even at three, I realized that things were changing. I watched the feedings with interest, and as the months went by, she'd look at me, smiling and cooing.

By the time she was a year old, she jumped up and down, peering at me from her crib, which fascinated me. I loved watching her jump and tried all the more to get her excited. The interaction was daily, but for brief periods, and then I went into my own comfortable fantasy world.

We had a swing set in the backyard, and I loved to swing. When Natalie was old enough to join me, I was glad. That's when I think I realized she could be my little companion. I taught her how to play as I did—not necessarily with toys, but with things. We collected rocks with unique shapes and colors. One of our favorite games was pulling each other across the floor on a blanket after Mom polished the floor. She was an eager little playmate; however, I only played with her for brief periods as we were growing up, then I'd retreat into my mind.

My mom's depression got bad at times, especially since one of her previous pregnancies had resulted in a stillbirth around the same time her mother died. She was sick every other year, but I never seemed to notice her absence very much as I retreated into my world. More and more, my poor little sister would cry and say I wouldn't play with her. I was confused, and I thought she was lying. It never occurred to me that I just didn't notice her until she got worked up. I suppose I also felt pressured by the fact that she needed me so. There must have been times when I retreated more, because I remember going through a period when I noticed her even less.

I compare these retreats into my world with the old TV series *Little Rascals*, where there were seldom any parents or adults around as the children went about their activities. Now just imagine one little rascal playing by himself, obliviously enjoying his little world, free of adults and other children. That's the best way I can explain the inside view of someone with AS. It's assumed adults and other children are there, but you really are in your mind and don't notice anything else. Getting interrupted is like going to a commercial break: most times it's upsetting and sometimes it's pleasant, depending on the type of interruption.

# Chapter 5

# Fascination with Human Nature

I always preferred the company of adults to the company of kids. Kids came on so strong, and it seemed to me that they had a whole different set of social rules. My fascination with human nature began when I was around six or so, and I always wanted to sit at the table to hear the adults talk while I studied them.

There were just a few cousins that I liked to be around. They visited often, so I knew what to expect with them. One in particular was Carl, my favorite little cousin. He was rambunctious, but he always started out his visit by being shy. It actually took at least fifteen minutes to get him to play. I would always start out by helping him remove his coat, and I loved to see the patterns on his sweater. This habit had become a ritual he even came to expect. His clothes smelled of fabric softener, and I looked forward to his familiar scent. Carl was fun, and we liked the same things. He had an active and interesting imagination. One of our favorite games was jumping from high places while we screamed. His main goal was to have as much fun as he possibly could, and I eagerly joined in.

My other cousins were over less often, but the ones who were quiet and reserved made me feel more comfortable. Julie was my age. She was pretty but unbelievably shy. I could almost feel her pain. She spoke in somewhat of a whisper, never touched her food at dinner, and later asked me to get her a snack to eat in private.

I felt safe with Julie and realized I wasn't alone with my internal struggles. Even at four years old, I instinctively knew she was worse off than I was.

I was becoming quite skilled at imitating others, especially if their personalities impressed me. My mother disapproved of my personality changes and uttered threats that I wouldn't see my cousins for a long time if I kept them up. If I saw a scenario on television, I would practice reenacting the scene, along with the drama, and use it in situations that related to mine. I became a talented actress, and I was proud. Eventually, I was assuming other personalities; they weren't totally real, but pieces of personalities that intrigued me. I was on my way to becoming what I thought people expected me to be: normal.

> I studied the various ways people responded and made them a part of my automatic repertoire. This was my way of coping with social situations, and it became a major part of my life. To this day, these responses and personalities have intertwined their way into my actual personality.

My first real obsession came around three months later. By this time, I simply adored horses and signed out library books on horses every chance I got. For years I asked my parents to get me a horse. My dad never said no, but simply responded with, "We'll see. Maybe someday." I never did get a horse. Although it was upsetting to always hear the same vague response, a small part of me is appreciative of the fact that I was never told I couldn't get one. It gave me hope that someday it could be a possibility.

It was when my grandfather came to live with us that my practiced responses and acting skills were most apparent. I called him Pepere. I was around five, and he came in from working outside. He complained about straining himself. He was breathing heavily and rubbing his chest, shoulder, and arm. He told my parents that his arm was numb. I was immediately concerned because even as a little girl, I recognized his symptoms from a program I saw on television. Coincidently, the program aired the night before. Due to my ability to remember unusual strings of information, I made the connection. His overall appearance bore an uncanny resemblance to the man I saw on TV having a heart attack. "Pepere, there's something wrong with your heart. I think you're having a heart attack," He smiled at me and said he just hurt himself outside. After much insisting, my parents took him to the hospital and, just as I suspected, he had suffered a minor heart attack.

He later sat down with me and asked me how I could know such a thing. "I saw it on TV," I replied. His question surprised and confused me because my response seemed logical enough. How could others not make the connection when we all saw the same program?

He smiled. "You could be my nurse from now on. I trust you more than a real nurse, and I know you'll help a lot of people someday."

I believe that this was one of the factors contributing to my interest in health and helping others with all the information I absorbed from television and books. I never did enter the health field, because I don't like seeing people suffer. I know this sounds insensitive, but I especially don't like hearing people complain, which is a problem I have with empathy. Nonetheless, to this day I can pinpoint the possible causes of symptoms. Because health is one of my deep-seated interests, I am able to retain this type of knowledge.

For as long as I can remember, I've had a tendency to run on and on about certain subjects, especially if it relates to the person I'm speaking to. I'll drone on with as much information as possible with the idea that the person has a right to all the information relating to his or her condition. I have to watch for indications that they want to change the subject. At first they seem visibly interested, but after too much information they seem to get bored, and I clumsily try to change the subject.

# Chapter 6

## Escape from School Anxieties

As a five year old, I felt extreme anxiety about going to school. I also saw this in Josh. I couldn't stand how lost and frightened I felt, and I quickly learned to escape by picturing myself at home. This was the only way I could hold myself together.

> I always drew the same picture of our house and paid particular attention to the kitchen window, drawing in the pretty curtains. It made me feel secure, and I imagined being inside.

I'd spend hours in class imagining I was sitting on the kitchen floor, looking up at the window as the sun shone onto the blue and yellow tiles or watching my mom at the kitchen counter as she baked and hummed. I felt really secure, as though I were in a state of hypnosis, totally oblivious to the sights and sounds of my environment. I was really there at home, safe and sound.

All of a sudden, I'd be yanked out of my dream state by a rude interruption. The teacher and kids would be shouting my name like the blast of a loud-speaker. I couldn't believe how loud their voices were, and the teacher would ask me why I wasn't answering when she called my name over and over.

I answered in confusion. "You were calling me?"

"Yes, I called you six times. Why didn't you answer?"

I felt both annoyed and embarrassed. I really didn't hear them and didn't understand why they were so angry with me. It was like being asleep and waking out of a dream.

On parent-teacher nights and on all my report cards, teachers commented on how I always daydreamed. They said I had trouble expressing myself and wasn't performing to my capabilities. I couldn't understand or even control it; I was labeled a lazy kid and eventually began believing it. After all, adults knew everything. My parents had serious talks with me about paying attention in class. I promised them I wouldn't daydream anymore and wondered how exactly I was going do that. It was peaceful and warm in my world, and I loved to do the things that I enjoyed.

One day, I was in dream mode when the teacher and kids managed to get my attention. Pointing out to the window the teacher said, "Sophia, the little green aliens were just here asking for you."

In a state of confusion, I stood to look toward the window, and all I heard was a loud roar of laughter. They all laughed at me, including the teacher. I sat down and tried to laugh, but I couldn't. I felt dizzy and sick to my stomach. I was so angry with all of them, including myself, and I was determined not to let them see me cry. Why couldn't I be like the others? It was bad enough that my mind controlled me at night; as hard as I tried, I couldn't control it during the day.

I occasionally had crying fits if I wasn't warned the night before that the next day was a school day. One Easter Sunday we got to church late and the parking lot was full. My dad turned around to park next door at my school. I looked out the window to see that we were parked beside the school entrance. I couldn't breathe for the life of me. I went into state of panic, screaming and crying uncontrollably.

"I don't want to go to school! It's not a school day; today's Sunday!" Determined, I held on to my seat, expecting to be picked up and taken to class. I didn't want to go to school.

There was always something very strange about my sense of humor. I found the most inappropriate things to be funny. There are two instances of inappropriate humor that really stayed with me, and you'll soon understand why. I must have been around six when I saw a Sylvester and Tweety cartoon episode where the cat falls down the stairs and gets flattened by a piano thrown down by Tweety. It was hilarious to me, and I sat there laughing until my gray and white cat walked by.

I wanted to reenact the scene I just saw, so I grabbed my cat, threw him down the stairs. The poor cat fell directly on his head and suffered so much he had to be put down. Everyone thought I was trying to test the theory that a cat always lands on its feet. I felt really bad about what I did, and I realized what was happening as a result, but I didn't feel sad about losing him. It was more like regret. That day, I learned how fragile life could be and never did anything like it again.

Another example of inappropriate humor was where I and a large group of kids were waiting for the school bus one morning. Gary, a boy who lived across the street from me—a nice, though hyperactive kid—got excited at seeing a tractor go by. He ran behind it for a ways but then veered off into traffic, where he was instantly hit by a car. He flew over fifteen feet in the air and landed headfirst on the pavement.

There was nothing I could do to stop from laughing. I wasn't nervous; quite the opposite. I found it as comical as a cartoon, even though no one else was laughing. Some kids were crying, and others were yelling at me to stop laughing. I still couldn't control myself until I saw the puddle of blood and realized just how serious it was. Surprisingly, Gary managed to stand up. I watched the driver ask him if he was all right. The driver then sat him down on the side of the road as though nothing happened, got into his car, and left. Gary's brother Mike and my brother Marc carried him to his house. I followed them and watched as they took him into the house. Gary ended up with permanent brain injury and was never the same again. Even now, if I see someone trip and fall, as long as there is no injury, it's often quite difficult for me to keep a straight face. As a result of this, the kids gave me a hard time that year. They said I was weird, and the bus ride and school became all the more stressful for me.

By the time I got to school, I was exhausted. When the teacher spoke, it sounded like a loud echo in a tunnel, which gave me headaches. I couldn't understand why the teacher's voice had to be so loud. It was aggravating. My parents used to say it was because she had to make sure everyone could hear her. But to me, she sounded like a foghorn in a tunnel, and I worried all the more that something was wrong with me. The stress was unbelievable. I hoped against all hope that she wouldn't ask me a question, because when she did, I said nothing. How could I answer a question when I only heard part, if any of it? She'd get upset with me and insist on getting an answer. I didn't hear her question, and even if I did, I couldn't come up with an answer. Her words only came in waves, and I never knew the whole story.

Each and every day was a struggle to keep a low profile. I was often misunderstood due to faking or, I should say, exaggerating stomachaches. I was proud of my new skill because it was my way of coping, but at the same time I was also ashamed. My parents eventually caught on after several visits to the doctor's office, and I confided that I didn't want to go to school. "School's too hard; I never know what I'm supposed to do! My stomach doesn't really hurt, but it feels awful when I'm at school." From then on, my teacher would allow me to lie down in the sick room, and I heard them say I had a nervous stomach. It amazed me how they figured out what I could never begin to put into words. I lay there wondering if I was going to have a nervous stomach forever, or if it was only going to happen at school. No one else seemed to feel the way I did. I realized and accepted that I was the girl with the nervous stomach.

All through grade school, I was behind and always the last to finish my work. I always wondered how the other students could understand what was asked of them and start their work so easily while I sat there waiting to have it explained to me again. I longed to be like other kids. I just hoped and wished I would soon grow into normalcy.

The fact that I was left-handed didn't help matters any. Left-handed writing was either discouraged or not allowed thirty-five years ago, and the teachers' constant scowls of disapproval throughout grade school discouraged me. I finally found a trick to remember my left from my right at the end of first grade. My left hand faced the window and my right faced the blackboard. I came into the classroom one day to discover that the desks had been reorganized to face the back. I was writing with my left hand, thinking it was my right, and got excited that it was working out for me. Unfortunately, I was once again reprimanded, and my excitement was replaced with anger and a feeling of utter stupidity. At times, I still have to briefly look at my hand before giving someone directions; it's not a natural thing for me. I also have difficulty with sense of direction. Finding my way back, even if I've been to a location several times before, is still quite challenging for me.

My second grade teacher, Mrs. Messier, changed my outlook. She was sweet and delicate. She spoke tenderly, and I had a feeling she understood me. I saw the concern in all that she did and in the way she gently explained something to me so that I could understand. She actually made me feel like crying with relief. Finally, I could stop feeling like a jumble of nerves when I was in class. Mrs. Messier spoke to my parents about her concerns, but unlike the other teachers, who insisted I was lazy and preferred to day-dream, she urged them to have me see a doctor. We sat in the doctor's office while my mother explained my tendency to daydream and my inability to fully understand instructions. She also brought my report cards to show him the consistency in each teacher's comments. It turned out that the doc-tor couldn't determine what was wrong. He chalked it up to extreme shy-ness and a nervous stomach and insisted I would grow out of it.

The rest of the year was easier for me, but I still worried about next year—or worse, that something horrible would happen to Mrs. Messier and I would have to endure a replacement teacher. It's amazing how I wor-ried about people dying, but it didn't affect me in the way you would expect. My biggest worry was dealing with the changes that would inevitably come with the finality of their death.

Recess was lonely and uncomfortable for me. I stood alone against the wall, wondering how the other kids could just run and have fun. The sun was so bright that squinting was a necessity for me, which made me an easy target for teasing. One boy in particular would imitate my facial expressions and then punch me in the stomach so hard I couldn't breathe. Thankfully, the nice kids would come to my rescue. They'd hold my hand and lead me to their group. I simply stood with them without saying a word as I watched them play. It seemed to come so naturally to them, and they looked confident. I wanted to be included, but I didn't know how to start, so I stood and watched.

When my sister, Natalie, started school, it was pure relief for me. She stood outside with me as I watched over her. Just her presence made my surroundings easier to cope with. If anyone hurt or teased her, I felt an overwhelming urge to protect her, and to my amazement, I chased them away like a lioness protecting her cub.

This gave me a feeling of power and confidence I had never experienced before. I secretly hoped for a situation to arise so I could stand up to the bullies and threaten them once again. This always shocked them into stepping down and, surprisingly, I never got into serious trouble.

At the end of fifth grade, I learned to socialize more. I came out of my shell, so to speak. It took me the full school year to get comfortable enough to laugh at jokes or mutter comments, which surprised everyone around me. They'd basically look around, asking, "Who said that?"

The others would say, "It was Sophia!"

Some kids actually tried to encourage me, while others commented, "She can actually speak?"

I was amazed at how good it felt to be noticed, and I continued to make more efforts to socialize by forcing myself to speak

I always got nervous before speaking. I knew I had to force myself, so I'd tell myself to *take a deep breath and say something. Then you can't back out, and the rest will take care of itself.*

That wasn't always the best way to do it, but it usually got me results. At other times, I said something totally inappropriate or ill-timed.

One of the girls in my neighborhood included me in the soccer games they played at recess and lunch. The rules were straightforward, and to my surprise, I played soccer well. I didn't have to say anything, and I charged forward with the ball. People got out of the way to avoid getting hurt, and I was quickly considered a valuable player.

It wasn't about the competition for me. I was just pleased to be included. It felt great to be one of the first kids picked on the team. I found myself getting more and more comfortable, and I laughed out loud at funny situations.

# Chapter 7

# Peer Manipulations

It was always easy for others to influence me, and I found myself in situations where I didn't know what to do. People seemed to spot my vulnerabilities and were quick to take advantage of me. Gary's older brother Mike hung out with my brother Marc, and he molested me at least once a week. It began when I was eight. He'd trick my brother into going upstairs long enough for him to get busy with me before I could think of a way out of the situation. I was riddled with shame and blamed myself as much as I did him. All I had to do was walk away, but I didn't. It was too late. Although it was uncomfortable, the molestations had become a routine, and I no longer cared. More than anything, I didn't want anyone to find out. It mysteriously stopped when I was eleven, and I felt free again. I was finally free of the humiliation, but the guilt and shame remained.

The neighborhood boys were very cruel. They'd tease me and call me "It." Natalie was "It's sister." They did this every time they saw us—on the bus, at school, and even if I sat outside in the front yard. They lived right across from our house. There were two brothers, Mike and Andrew, and the worst was Brady, another kid next door. I often wondered what would make them tease me that way. They said it with such contempt, I can only rationalize that they saw something strange in me. If I could pinpoint what it was, I'd say it was because I couldn't really keep up with their conversations. If they sarcastically asked me what I thought, I'd either draw a blank or say something completely off-topic. I used to try to study them so that I could learn how to act or what to say, which probably seemed creepy to them. That's my only explanation for the teasing. The bottom line is they made me feel like a freak.

I started puberty when I was twelve, and Mike, Andrew, and Brady finally showed what I thought was a new respect towards me. They befriended me and asked me if I'd go on a roller-skating date with them, which was confusing. Asking me to go on a date was strange enough, but going on a date with them was unthinkable. Nevertheless, I was finally glad to be accepted. I started hanging out with them, and they said I had to wait until I was more mature if I was to go with them. I must have seemed immature to them because the date still didn't happen. That summer, they started a small boy band. They played guitar and drums, and I watched their sessions. It was so nice to not be teased anymore. I was simply astonished when Andrew asked me to go out on a date later that summer to the roller skating arena. Andrew was a year older than me and never seemed as eager as the others during their teasing phase; rather, he often remained quiet through it all. I was filled with excitement and relief. The thought of being considered worthy of their friendship was a personal milestone for me. However, I quickly learned there was a price to pay. If it meant no more teasing and finally belonging, I was willing to take that chance.

It started gradually. They began teasing me about stuffing my bra. Andrew said he wouldn't go on a date with me if I didn't prove them wrong. After several weeks of teasing, I finally gave in and agreed to show them my newly budding breasts. Only, that wasn't enough. We were in a field by the creek behind the cabin we built. They pressured and taunted me to show more. When I resisted, they scoffed and said that they knew I wasn't mature enough to show anything else. I took a deep breath and took their dare. The three of them stood in a semicircle in front of me, gawking at me and urging me to continue. I felt sick and nervous and tried to drown out their disgusting comments with my own thoughts as I removed my clothes. They grew quiet and looked at me. They started to touch me, and just then, Natalie walked in on the whole thing, and I quickly grabbed my clothes to cover up. I was numb; my mind spun out of control as I tried to figure out what to do. Usually, whenever we got caught doing something, we'd tell them to join us and that way they couldn't tell on us. I said the first thing that came to my mind. "Join us, Natalie. You'll see— it'll be fun!" I realize now that I couldn't seem to relate to anyone else's feelings but my own.

The thought of how humiliating or damaging it could have been for her never crossed my mind. I'm thankful to say that she was so upset and embarrassed she ran off. I quickly dressed and felt sick to my stomach at the thought that I would be found out. I didn't have the energy to deal with it. I felt myself giving up inside and decided to deal with the consequences later. The humiliation was so great, I retreated to the cabin and sat there huddled up in a corner. I wondered how she could be so smart and levelheaded. At the same time, I was angry with myself for not walking away. I definitely didn't need them. They were idiots. I was glad the date didn't happen. Natalie never mentioned a word about that day to me or to my parents.

> That's when I realized my sister only did what she believed in, and I found a deep admiration for her in that moment. I realized I shouldn't have to try to please everybody in order to get accepted.

I took a page out of her book and stopped hanging out with them. Unfortunately, the teasing started again. Instead of using a repulsed tone, they used a more playful tone, and the name "It" had been replaced with "Lips." I avoided them at all costs by staying inside, watching a lot of television, and reading. Natalie taught me a valuable lesson that day. Although I regret the confusion and humiliation I caused her, I have to say, in a way I'm glad she came by when she did. Otherwise, I don't want to think about what might have happened. Without realizing it, she actually saved me from making a series of dangerous mistakes.

A week had passed and I was sick with a urinary tract infection, which had gone to my kidneys. I was in terrible pain, and my parents urged me to tell them what happened. I couldn't tell them what I did; they would never look at me the same way again. I had an overwhelming urge to confide the secret I'd been keeping bottled up inside about the three years of molestations. I knew Brady didn't cause the infection because it hadn't occurred in over a year. This just happened to be the perfect opportunity to expose him for taking away my innocence, and I took it. I told my mother about what happened, and I was careful not to give out too many details. Part of my confession was a lie. I was consumed with guilt, but at the same time I felt tremendous relief. Marc was confused by the whole ordeal; he often questioned me and suspected me of lying, but he still wasn't sure. Brady was charged with molesting a minor.

I was filled with pride. I took control of my destiny for a change, and to my relief, the teasing suddenly ended.

This is a poem I later wrote to express my thoughts and emotions.

### Emergence

Forever in a void of nothingness,
So lonely, misunderstood.
Nowhere to go,
A heavy heart.
Missing pieces,
Loss for words.
Don't know how to begin,
Take a deep breath, let it all out.

I have inadvertently used an hourglass shape representing the sands of time, the various stages of my life, and my eventual search for belonging and emotional release.

# Chapter 8

# Family Ties

I had really grown attached to my brothers and looked up to all of them. My brother Ron is ten years older than I am. He moved away when he was seventeen. It's a shame that we didn't get to spend a lot of time together as children, but we're closer now as adults. He's best described as the strong, independent type with a big heart. He never did tolerate unfairness and was quick to defend anyone, especially his mother and siblings. He is passionate about what he believes in and, much like a bear, he can be sweet and cuddly one minute and easily infuriated the next.

My brother Rick would be best described as gentle and remarkably talented. He skillfully played guitar and just needed to hear a song a few times to play it by ear. He was good-looking, very intelligent, and just had an amazing memory. I loved singing while he played, and we eventually practiced doing the same two songs each and every day until we mastered them. He seemed to really enjoy the fact that I took such interest in his hobby. He taught me how to style my hair, told me what I should wear, and gave me advice whether I wanted it or not. Our bond was strong, and he was proud to tell me I was beautiful. He even had me practice walking with a book on my head and showed me off to his girlfriend.

My brother Marc was another great influence in my life. He's the total opposite of my brother Ron. He rarely got angry, but when he did, it was like a total loss of control. I can literally count on one hand the number of times I saw him angry. We have a lot in common—not words, but a state of being. Growing up with him was a soothing experience. He and I spent many hours playing with his farm animals and yes, with the doorstop. We went blueberry picking, but instead of picking berries we were happier exploring. His patience was abundant. He always showed me the best methods, or tricks, as he would say, for just about everything from home-work to fishing. The way I see it, he's a diamond in the rough; he has great potential to invent new products by improving on existing inventions, and then again, it's never too late. For as long as I've known Marc, he's always tried and succeeded in finding much better ways of doing anything.

Having three older brothers has been a real plus for me. Watching them inter-act has been instru-mental in helping me figure out how to socialize with others.

The strangest thing about our relationship is, we never argued. They were supportive of me, even though none of us knew exactly what to make of my unique challenges. I will always be grateful for their love and espe-cially for their guidance.

# Chapter 9

# Obsessive Relationships

We had a cottage an hour away from home. We spent weekends and summers there, and I loved going. My father and three brothers built our cottage while we stayed in a tent. I loved camping; we'd wake up to the smell of bacon and eggs cooking on the old gas stove, the sounds of birds chirping, and the smell of freshly cut wood.

Our neighbors were a family of five girls, and I became friends with the girls near my age. Our friendship began when I was about nine years old. Laurie reminded me of my cousin Julie. She and her sister Rebecca competed for my attention. It was wonderful to feel needed, but at the same time I felt smothered and caught in the middle. They didn't understand my need for space, which I now realize might have created somewhat of a challenge to their competitive nature. They never took no for an answer and always ended up convincing me to come out with them. I wound up giving in to Laurie and Rebecca's pleas, which was quite exhausting at times. I was with them from morning till night, and I eventually got used to the dynamics of relationships—not to mention sibling rivalry.

It hadn't occurred to me that having friends would be such a commitment. I just wanted to stay in my room so I could immerse myself in my collection of *Archie* comic books. I read often, and *Archie* was one of the best tools for learning most of the cues of socializing. To me, reading the comics was like being part of their group without the pressures of making friends. I liked Betty's character, and many of my qualities were borrowed from her. I envied their relationships and longed for the same type of acceptance and dynamics they had. Over time, I adopted personality traits from other role models such as Linda Carter on Wonder Woman and Jacqueline Smith on Charlie's Angels.

Looking back, I can actually say with conviction that Laurie and Rebecca really helped me socially prepare for the future. We had fun. We sang, baked, had sleepovers, and yes, we even had fights. My friends, however, told it like it was. They were brutally honest, and of course it was easy to manipulate me into doing what they wanted. "You're so weird!" they'd say, and explain to me what to do or not do. When they introduced me to their other friends, I never knew what to say, so I usually stood silently on the sidelines listening to their conversations. Laurie and Rebecca would tell me I could have at least asked them questions. At the end of the day, we remained friends.

I met my best friend, Jessica, through them. She stayed in a nearby cottage as well. She also happened to live in the same city as I did. We felt an immediate connection. We were inseparable at the cottage as well as in the city. She was shy and petite, and I felt she needed to be taken care of. She liked the same things I did. We listened to music, sang, hung out, and talked about boys. Sometimes we didn't talk at all. Unlike Laurie and Rebecca, Jessica never had any expectations of me; our relationship was based on give and take, which was the complete opposite of what I was used to.

We had something else in common, which happened to be a crush on the cutest guy we ever set our eyes on. His name was Ben, and we were crazy about him. He had a cottage at the end of our bay and also lived in our city. He had blond hair, blue eyes, and was twelve years old. We competed for his attention, and everybody could tell that he liked me most. He was shy and sweet in a cool sort of way, and he rode a dirt bike. We adored him, and we always took walks down the cottage dirt road in hopes of seeing him.

Within a couple of days, he gave me a ride on his bike. I rode behind him with my arms around his waist, and I could smell the fresh country air in his hair. I felt like I was in heaven. I was wearing shorts and burned the inside of my calf on the motor. To my surprise, the burn took on the shape of a heart and didn't hurt as much as I expected. After that, I drew hearts everywhere, and to this day I still notice them in the oddest places—etched in concrete or hidden in marble patterns or water stains. When I see a heart-shaped pattern, even today, I'm overjoyed. Ben gave me his phone number and asked me to go out with him. I was on top of the world. I called him almost every night, but I didn't quite know what to talk about, and he wasn't much of a talker himself.

Two months after, he grew tired of me and would cut our calls short. Then he started to refuse my calls or hang up on me. I would have rejected me, too. I was fixated on him, and there was nothing he could do to shake me off. The fixation became an obsession, and I relentlessly pursued him every day for almost a year. I got very depressed, to say the least, but Jessica was always there to offer me words of encouragement.

# Chapter 10

## Deceptions of a Girl Named Sylvia

A year had passed since I met Jessica and Ben. I was sitting at the kitchen table finishing my homework as Jessica patiently sat next to me. All I remember was raising my pencil and waking up on a hospital stretcher. I had suffered a grand mal seizure and scared the hell out of her and my family. I was convulsing uncontrollably for over fifteen minutes.

The neurologist told me I had epilepsy, which disappointed and confused me. He gave me strict instructions as to what I could and could no longer do. He said I could no longer be alone. The activities I took for granted, like canoeing, swimming, and cycling were now too dangerous. The solitude I so valued was being taken from me and replaced with constant surveillance. My world was coming apart—Ben hated me, and I had lost my independence and had to be on medication for the rest of my life. Needless to say, I was not a lot of fun to be around.

I was depressed and heavily medicated, but Jessica still stood by me through it all. She tried everything to cheer me up, and she had the idea to call the party line, which was a lot like an online chat room where you can talk to all kinds of people. Only it was on a local phone line that only people in the area would be on. I asked people the same questions: What's your name? What school do you go to? Do you know so-and-so? What type of music do you listen to? This was as far as I comfortably got, and I hoped the rest would take care of itself.

I used the party line just long enough to be manipulated by a girl named Sylvia. She went to my school and told me her brother was Len

Crouse, the most popular boy in grade eight. He was tall and blond and looked a lot older than he was. Spring break had arrived, and I figured I had nothing to lose. I made plans to meet Sylvia and Len at noon so we would go to the arcade. I was excited and scared. Just to think I could get him to notice me was good enough for me.

When I got there, Sylvia was there, but she said something had come up and he couldn't make it. I was disappointed, but then she said he was going to call me that night. I was thrilled about that and spent the day with her. That night, just as she promised, Len called me. I was nervous, but he made me feel secure with his reassuring voice. He was nothing like I imagined.

He called me every other day and even sang to me. My confidence soared. He was the nicest guy I'd ever talked to, and I couldn't wait to actually meet up with him. I never understood why something came up whenever we tried to see each other, but I looked forward to his calls. I saw him one day at school and called out his name. He smiled at me, and when I approached him and started talking to him, he looked confused and acted like he didn't even know me. He basically told me he had to go, and he left.

Later that day, I saw Sylvia. She said she had to talk to me about something important and would come over after dinner. I worried that she was going to tell me that her brother was breaking up with me. We stood out in the driveway as I anxiously waited for her to speak. She looked sad and put her arms around me, no doubt to comfort me. To my surprise, she kissed me. I was taken by surprise and pulled away. She confessed to being in love with me and admitted to impersonating her brother Len. She went on to say he wasn't her brother and that this was the only way she could think of to get to know me. I was reeling with what she just said to me—partly because I felt like he'd died, and also because I'd lost the friend I thought I had. I was disgusted and told her to leave me alone. I was filled with anger and resentment, and I got really depressed.

Sylvia was persistent. She called me and came over, begging me to forgive her. She said she didn't want to lose me as a friend, and in the vulnerable state that I was in, I eventually caved. After a while, I ended up being intimate with her, and I became repulsed with myself. It took me over three months to finally confess this to my parents. They didn't even look shocked about it. They assured me that it was only a phase that many people go through but never admit. I tried to convince them that it was more than that, or I wouldn't have told them.

It took me a good while to come to terms with my sexuality. Eventually I realized that this was a phase, and that it was time to cut all ties with Sylvia.

I never expected her to react the way she did. She was wild with vengeance. Sylvia always talked about how tight she was with the Weston Street gang, and now she threatened to have them beat me up. I could see she was serious. She vowed to make my life a living hell. I was upset and frightened at the thought of what she meant by that, and I tried to convince myself not to let her get the best of me. It was no use; I felt myself sinking into a depression.

# Chapter 11

# Final Moments

I was thirteen years old and at an all-time low. I hated my very existence and decided that day would be my last. No one could ever hurt me again. I spoke to Jessica on the phone that day and told her, as I had many times before, that I wished I were dead. I grabbed all my pills and my father's as well. I headed out to the old underground cabin the neighborhood boys had made. It hadn't been used in years, and I knew I would never be found there alive. I forgot to bring water, so I swallowed two and a half bottles of pills dry for fear that my plan would be foiled. I had never felt such desperation as I did at that moment. Strangely, I felt relief that soon my existence would be over. I cried out to God, asking him why I had to be born. Life was so hard for me, and now I had to do the hardest thing imaginable. I was forced to put my family through unimaginable anguish. The very idea of ending my pain far outweighed the pain I knew I would be causing my family and all the people I loved.

It didn't take long. I felt weak, and as I fell into darkness, it occurred to me that I'd never grow up and have children. They would love me unconditionally and accept me as I was. It occurred to me that I wanted to live. I tried to scream over and over again, but nothing came out. I couldn't move, and I prayed to God not to let me die. *Please give me another chance so I can grow and lead a normal life. I know I can!* I prayed until I no longer could and was left to die.

It was late at night, and everyone was out searching. They had looked everywhere, called everyone I knew, and nothing. For some reason, my dad thought of the old underground cabin. Somehow, he found me in the nick of time; any later would have been too late.

I woke up in the hospital to see my parents crying. They were hurt, angry, and relieved, and I knew I could never put them through this again. I was so drugged-up I couldn't even think. I felt totally helpless. It was difficult to put into words why I couldn't cope with life. It sounded ridiculous to me as I heard myself explain it to my parents. "I find life so hard. It's all the little things combined together, and it overwhelms me."

"What sort of things do you mean? You can tell us anything."

"Pressures from schoolwork. The pills I have to take for my epilepsy make me drowsy and I've lost so much freedom because of it. Ben can't stand me because I really screwed up and wouldn't leave him alone." I just felt like I was a mistake and should never have been born.

I was in the hospital psychiatric ward for several weeks. I saw a psychiatrist, who accused me of lying to him. He didn't believe that I could find life so difficult without a valid reason, as he put it. I wanted help with my personal struggles, but all he did was reprimand me and try to make me promise I wouldn't do it again. That was like making me promise I would be able to handle it the next time I experienced the overwhelming helplessness that so often plagued me. I didn't know how to explain how I felt. He tried to play on my shame. He lied to me about my parents paying him by the hour and said I'd better start talking. I didn't know it then, but the psychiatrist was covered under their health plan. In order to get him off my back, I lied and told him that it was because of drugs and peer pressure.

He believed me immediately and, with a smug look of satisfaction, he replied, "Now we're making progress." If I continued to do so, I would be able to go home sooner. I sat there in front of him, answering his questions with more lies until the sessions ended.

If it wasn't bad enough that I was depressed and drugged-up from all the pills in my system, the orderly was kissing and touching me. All I could do was silently cry. I was so ashamed that I said nothing. I didn't dare tell the doctor, only to be accused of more lies. During the day, the orderly played board games with me and encouraged me to be cheerful if I wanted to be released. I played board games with him, faked a smile, and tried to act like I was in a good mood so that I would be released. It worked. A week later, I was home. He had the nerve to call me at home, and I told him to leave me alone. He never called me again.

The whole ordeal was more than I could take. I was exhausted and fell into a deeper depression. I actually wished I hadn't been found. Each day took me deeper into feelings of utter hopelessness. Two weeks later, I tried to end my life again. I can't recall exactly what triggered it, but this time I found myself in our basement cold cellar, swallowing more pills. I figured by the time they searched everywhere else, it would be too late and my struggles would be over. My desperation was so strong I blocked any thoughts of how traumatizing it would have been for them to find me that way.

Apparently, my brother Marc found me. He cried for help, and once again I woke up in the hospital. The doctor started in on me again about how it didn't make any sense for me to be so depressed and insisted I come out with it. I told him I regretted my attempts and promised to never do it again. I told more lies, assumed my cheerful disposition again, and was released within a few days. As I look back on that experience, I'm not sure if the doctor suggested medication for depression (I may have refused because of the effects of my other medications). Things would have been much easier for me if he had.

When my brother Rick found out about the suicide attempts, he was disappointed in me and confused about the reason I gave. That year, I had made a promise to him to stay away from drugs. I think he felt bad about the idea that I tried to kill myself as a result. It was the only reason I could think of at the time. Although it was a lame excuse, it was more believable than the reality of it all. Nevertheless, I took promises seriously.

If anyone tried to pressure me into giving in, I used the excuse Rick suggested. "Tell them you're allergic to smoke." It worked.

People were kind, but they tended to exclude me, which was perfect. The people I wanted to be with didn't use drugs, except for Ben. That could have been the reason he felt uncomfortable with me.

# Chapter 12

# Family Tragedy

I spent a lot of time in my room listening to the albums my brother Rick gave me. I was fourteen at the time and missed our jam sessions together; singing with him as he played his guitar made me feel connected to myself, to him, and to life. He moved out of town shortly after he married Pam, a short, stout woman. They were expecting their first child. She was the type of person who would examine situations and manage to find countless ways of using them to her advantage by controlling the events and people around her. They were, in my opinion, a poor match. She was selfish and manipulative, and Rick was selfless and giving. After our cousin Claude's apartment burned down, Rick took him in until Claude got back on his feet. Rick's kindness was inspiring, and he never expected anything in return.

One morning in May, my parents woke me to terrible news. My dad was sitting on the edge of my bed, stirring me out of my sleep. "Sophia? Wake up, Cherie." I was surprised at how gentle he was. Normally he pulled on my toes to wake me up. "Rick was in a car accident last night," he said, looking at me carefully.

Between yawns, I asked him where he was, and my dad replied that he was in the hospital. I asked if Rick was okay.

He let out a small cry and said, "No, Sophia, he's not okay. He didn't make it!" He held me and sobbed.

I will never forget that moment; it's etched in my mind and my heart. My world came crashing down as I cried out, "No, not Rick!" This had to be a bad dream. He held me as I cried, and over his shoulder I saw my mom crying and holding my pills and a glass of water. I looked down and saw my legs shaking. She quickly gave me my pills, managed to soothe me, and succeeded in preventing a seizure.

My mom was holding my sister, and I could see the intense pain in their faces as we cried together. I got up to go to the kitchen, and what I saw was too much to bear. My brother Marc, who is only a year younger than Rick, stood with a blank expression on his face.

"My sweet little Marc," Mom said as she wrapped her arms around him. "It's okay to cry, Marc. Go ahead and cry," she pleaded.

Then he collapsed into the hardest, most broken-up sobs I've ever seen. Never had I witnessed such devastation pouring out of a human soul.

Just as that was happening, my oldest brother Ron came in. He took off his shoes and slowly walked into the kitchen with grief in his voice as he cried out, "My little brother's gone. He's gone, and I never got to tell him how I loved him." Like a child, he walked over to my mom and held her, crying on her shoulder.

We all held each other, and the next few days were a blur. All I could do to keep from feeling utterly and completely lost was to carry a picture of Rick.

My best friend, Jessica, took a week off of school and stayed by my side the entire time. She tried to cheer me up or change my ideas. We listened to music together and did what we always did, and that brought me comfort. I needed things to be the same, but if I stopped thinking about him for too long, I felt panic and guilt. I vowed to never let my memories of him fade, and I could not stop talking about him for fear that his presence would become only a faint memory. I pleaded for his spirit to visit me, and I was disappointed that he didn't. The more time passed, the more obsessed I became with keeping him alive. I was hurt if others didn't share in my quest. It was the hardest thing I'd ever had to go through, but I made it by dealing with my grief in the only way I knew.

Jessica and I were coming home from a walk. She was trying to distract me from my brother's burial which took place that afternoon. As we came through the front door, nothing could have prepared me for what I saw.

Pam and Claude were sitting together on our sofa, abruptly releasing each other from an intimate embrace. It was unbelievable.

"What the hell are you doing?" I shouted.

She looked down and replied, "You might as well know now. We're in love and have been for a while now."

I could taste the bile rising up in my throat and felt unsure of my footing. Something inside of me rose up, and the anger was more than I could bear. "Rick was just buried today! Look at you! You make me sick, you stupid bitch! Get out, now!"

She stayed seated and calmly held my gaze. In deliberate, even tones she replied, "I'm not leaving. Rick knew, and everyone else knew about it, for that matter. We were separating before he died. Sophia, you're going to have to accept it, especially if you want to keep peace for the baby's sake."

I was shaking uncontrollably. Jessica took me downstairs, trying her best to soothe me, but I kept thinking that I'd lost Rick, and now his manipulative wife was threatening to take the only part of him that remained. I was Desiree's godmother, and I realized I had to accept this nightmare if we didn't want to lose his baby, too. She was six weeks old and the only remaining connection to my brother.

> It went against every part of my being, but I kept the peace for the sake of the baby. I couldn't let his child grow up enduring a loveless, painful life.

The night before Rick died, my mother had found him in the guest room, holding the baby, pacing the floor, and sobbing. We later found out that he knew about the affair and that they were in the process of separating. Eventually, Pam confessed to the events leading to his death. Rick caught up with her and Claude at a local bar and told her he was leaving. He signed the car over to her and gave her the money in his wallet so she could have what she needed for the baby. He then asked her for some money back so he could catch the bus.

Out of anger, she refused. He took the keys and title and called my mom. He explained what had happened and that he was on his way home to stay with us. He drove off. A few miles later, one of his tires blew out.

He lost control of the car and landed in the ditch. Apparently, if it hadn't been for the fire hydrant he hit, he would have made it. I couldn't help thinking that she would have been the one in the car if she had given him the money for the bus.

The more time passed, the more obsessed I became with keeping his memory alive. I talked about him incessantly, reminiscing about the memories we shared, and I was hurt if others changed the subject or withdrew from my conversations.

I knew it hurt my family when I did this, but I was convinced that if they could keep his memory alive, they would be better off for it.

It was a long summer, and I was thankful I didn't have to deal with school. My mother ended up in the hospital with a breakdown, and I spent a lot of time walking by myself. I realized how lonely my sister must have been, but I had no strength to put forth much effort for her. Weekends were better. We went to the cottage, and it was calm and comforting.

# Chapter 13

# Guy Next Door

The end of the summer that year was quickly approaching, and my neighbor Julian was out on his dock again. He was sixteen years old and he was and so gorgeous, I found myself staring at him more often than was appropriate. He seemed to always be smiling, and I liked something about his way. There were always girls coming and going from his place, and I knew he was out of my league. I didn't have the confidence those girls had.

As always, I depended on Laurie and Rebecca to invite him to our campfire. He was playful and talkative; it was easy to get to know him. Once I felt comfortable enough, I told him about the kung fu classes I was taking, and he wanted me to teach him some of the moves.

I tried various moves, and none of them worked. He was solid, and he either blocked me or buckled my knees. It didn't go at all like it was supposed to, and we wound up laughing. I knew he liked me by the way he talked to me. Unfortunately, he ended up asking Rebecca to go out with him. I was surprised in a way, but she was older and it was amazing how easily she flirted. All she had to do was say something witty or sweet, and then giggle. It was like she was using a private language or something, and she was really good at it.

I watched her in action, and at times I found myself mimicking her flirting style.

One night, Julian showed up with Rebecca at one of our campfires. I couldn't help feeling guilty about being so attracted to my friend's boyfriend. I tried to look away, but I couldn't help myself. His presence demanded my attention. He picked up Rebecca's cat and playfully nuzzled its face with his own. I'm not sure how or why, but in that moment, Julian stole my heart.

That night, I lay awake in bed, amazed at the effect he had on me. I tried to block him out of my thoughts, but as hard as I tried, I couldn't. I'd gotten a glimpse of his sensitive side, and I knew I could fall in love with him. That's when I started to fantasize about kissing him.

It was only five months after Richard's death. I was finally starting to come to terms with losing him. I could talk about him without crying, but I couldn't control my voice from shaking when I mentioned his name.

My friends and I were hanging out at our usual campfire. The autumn air was cool that night. We all decided it would be a good time to celebrate before the cold weather set in. I needed to loosen up; it had been a horrible year. I suggested we get drunk, which was out of character for me, especially since I was only fourteen. It didn't take too much to convince the others, and we each snuck a few bottles from our parents.

It was Linda's idea to go in search of Ben. It didn't take much persuading at all for him to join in. Within an hour, we were all drunk and having a great time. We began walking down the dirt road which ran along the back of our cottage. It was dark, but the moon lit our way, which added to the ambiance. Julian showed up and hung out with us most of the night He wound up looking after me the entire time. Rebecca wasn't there that night. She had to babysit the neighbor's kids. Even though I was intoxicated, I was very aware of the fact that he'd opted to take care of me when he could have conveniently been alone with Rebecca while the kids slept. It puzzled me, but there was no denying how happy I was. The guilt I felt before was completely gone.

I knew I wouldn't be able to get him out of my mind for months. Logic told me that if something would happen between us, it would likely be a few years later. After all, he was two years older than I was. I knew he didn't go to the cottage during the winter months. Even though we lived in the same city, I knew that I wouldn't have had the courage to see him there.

The next morning, we were all on Rebecca's dock talking about the crazy night we'd had. Julian was teasing me about how I flirted with him and told him I loved him. Just then, I noticed my cousin Pat and his friend David on my dock, and I had a brilliant idea.

*What better way to get Julian to notice me? I'll swim over and talk to the new guy.* I figured it might just spark Julian into realizing he really wanted to be with me.

By the time I got there, I glanced back and noticed that Rebecca and Julian were gone. I was disappointed. My little scheme hadn't worked. *Or had it? Maybe he left because it bothered him.*

I decided to hope for the latter.

# Chapter 14

# First Relationships

I started to hang out with my cousin Pat. He was sweet, and I felt he filled the void Rick left. He had the same calm, intense demeanor my brother had, and it was a huge source of comfort to have him around. He and his friend David lived in a little town near out cottage. David was a kind and sensitive guy. He was shy, yet he was easy to talk to. I enjoyed his company. He was one of the only people I ever met who really knew how to listen and wanted to hear everything I had to say. It was surprising to me that it didn't make him uncomfortable to hear about my brother's death.

Two weeks after I met David, I decided to date him. He wasn't Julian, but we did have more in common with each other. I only saw him on weekends, which was perfect for me. I still had my own space, and I looked forward to our weekends together.

I felt more confident and made a few friends at school. I was in grade nine and met Donna, a petite blonde girl. She was sweet and quite pretty, and I thought she'd get along well with Pat. I was right. We all had a great time together. We went dancing each Saturday night and ended the night with our weekly ritual at a local restaurant for egg rolls and coffee.

David constantly shared his love for his favorite group, the Beatles. The passion he had when he spoke of them was admirable and somewhat intriguing. The band was considered old-fashioned by kids' standards at that time, but he didn't care. He proudly referred to them as his favorite group regardless of what others said to him. David constantly talked about our future together and his plans to someday get married and work as a train conductor. He was sweet, but things were getting too serious for me. I found myself feeling smothered and started realizing I wanted out of the relationship. Once I finally mustered the courage to break up with him, he pleaded with me to stay. This same scenario repeated itself several times. His pain was so intense that I couldn't go through with it until two years later. He was talking about getting married, and I knew I wasn't being fair to him.

Regardless of how nice he was, I couldn't stay with him, so I finally ended our relationship. The guilt was almost unbearable at first as I tried to get on with my life, and I promised myself never to get personally involved in a relationship unless I was ready.

He called me each and every day. I stood firm on my decision and insisted it wouldn't be fair to either of us to get back together. It was finally over. It was truly sad, but after all that time I couldn't feel pain, only relief at finding myself again.

That summer, spent again at the family cottage, I decided to go on a dating spree to make up for lost time. The years were good to me. I had grown from a kid with a big head and an awkward smile into an attractive sixteen year old with delicate features and long black hair. I made my intentions clear: I was just out to have a good time. As I look back at what I told every single guy, I now realize how a guy could have interpreted what I had said. However, my meaning was purely innocent. I didn't want anything to do with a long term commitment.

It was a beautiful Saturday morning in late July when Julian dropped in to borrow some eggs. He wore faded denim cutoffs and looked like one of those guys on a calendar with a bronze tan and a broad smile. "Hi! Do you have any eggs I can borrow?"

"Sure," I said. I pulled out two eggs from the refrigerator and handed them to him.

As he took them, he playfully looked at me and said, "I'm pretty hungry. I usually eat six eggs for breakfast."

I was puzzled but happy to oblige, and without a thought for tomorrow's breakfast, I grabbed four more and handed them to him.

"Hey," he continued, "why don't you come and join me? Later I'll take you out in the boat. We'll head out to town for ice cream."

I was careful not to look too eager. Even at this point, I really thought he was just being kind and his interest in me was simply platonic, or that maybe I alleviated his boredom.

With some persuasion, he convinced me to not only join him but jovially insisted I cook his breakfast. Little did he know that I had no clue how to cook an egg. I worried the whole time I was cooking them. I covered them with a lid, hoping they wouldn't stick. I was proud of myself. They looked fine. He started eating them, and the egg whites were runny and hung from his mouth. To my surprise, he didn't even comment and ate all six eggs. I watched him take bite after bite and was torn between staying quiet and telling him to leave them or he'd be sick. But I let him eat the disgusting breakfast I knew he'd never ask for again.

We spent the day together boating, and as he promised, we went to town for ice cream. We walked and talked; he teased me, and the day flew by.

We were sitting in his living room horsing around, which is something I always started if I didn't quite know what to do. Something came over me, and I laid a gentle kiss on his forehead.

He sat up, gave me a longing look, cupped my face with his hands, and kissed me so gently and passionately I felt weak. At the same time, I was nervous and hoped he enjoyed my kiss as much as I did his. I could see the effect my kiss had on him and felt like I could do no wrong. We kissed for hours that night, until it was getting late and I had to go. As I stood up to walk to the door, he playfully pinned me against the refrigerator door, and between kisses I heard him say, "I could marry you right now, you know that?" As he said it, a look of confusion came over him and left him speechless.

I walked home feeling content with myself as his words repeated themselves over and over in my mind. I was both happy and scared. I knew deep down I was in love. I was scared it would soon come to an end, so I decided not to let myself get too close. We saw each other every day for the following three weeks. I told him I wanted to be with him but I didn't want a serious relationship. He just cupped my face and said "Well, that's too bad, because I love you!"

"No!" I told him. "Don't say that!"

He'd repeat it over and over: "I love you!" I'd never experienced such euphoria before now; it was like waking out of a dream, and time stood still.

He walked me home one night, placed his hands on each side of my face and wrapped my hair around his fingers. "You are so beautiful, you know that? I always thought you looked like a little Gypsy girl with your long black hair and mysterious look."

"Really?" I asked, surprised. "What do you mean by mysterious look?"

He gently replied, "You have this intense look that's sort of wild, tender, and mysterious all at the same time."

It was late at night and he was going home. As always, we kissed until it was time to go. "Will you marry me?" he whispered as we stood outside the front door. I couldn't believe what he'd just asked me, and I asked him to repeat it in case I misunderstood. He said he wanted me to be his wife. I giggled and replied, "We're too young to even think about that. Our parents would have a fit."

He looked at me with a menacing look on his face. "They won't know anything. We won't tell them!" He had a look of quiet confidence, and there was a daring quality to the way he said that.

I laughed. He looked so sweet, and I had a feeling he got whatever he wanted, so I said, "Get that out of your head. You know we're too young to even go there. I'm only sixteen." He gave me a longing look and kissed me with an intensity that penetrated me.

The following morning, there was something different about him. His eyes were swollen, and he was quiet for the most of the day. I asked him if he was all right, and he just said he was tired. I was tired, too; it took me at least three hours to fall asleep. I kept fantasizing about being his wife. I had a feeling he was upset, but I still couldn't be sure. As the day went by and after much probing on my part, he admitted to being disappointed about the night before.

That night was the twenty-first of August, and my parents were throwing their annual outdoor party. We wanted to be alone together, so we went for a drive down the country road to a field nearby. It was a beautiful summer night, and you could see half a mile away with the bright, moonlit glow. He parked the car and sat looking at me, searching for the right moment. As if I could read his mind, I knew what he wanted to ask me. He was so beautiful, and I wanted to absorb every bit of this moment. I watched his lips form the words as he spoke.

"I love you, Babe. I want to spend every day of my life with you. I want you to be my wife. Marry me!"

I took a deep breath and said, "Yes, I want to be your wife more than anything in this world."

Just then he grabbed me hard, kissed me as if trying to reach inside of me, and said, "Yes, you're going to be my wife, and I want the world to know it."

"We really should keep this quiet for now," I said.

He started the car and headed to the little town nearby, and he beeped the horn and shouted for all to hear, "She said yes! She's going to be my wife! I'm the luckiest guy in the world!"

My euphoria was intoxicating. He was shouting it out for all to hear, and I didn't care. We talked excitedly about our future. We veered off onto a side street when we saw an old man in his long underwear standing on his front porch with a pad and pencil, taking down our license plate number. We giggled, turned around, and headed back to the field, where we talked about keeping it quiet for a few years.

We knew our parents wouldn't be ready to hear we were so young and in love, and we were satisfied with that. Julian laid out a blanket to sit on, and we kissed in the moonlight. It was so romantic. I couldn't keep myself from looking at him. The moonlight cast a silver glow, and shadows danced across his beautiful face. He fumbled for a moment, then, he held out a beautiful diamond studded engagement ring and placed it on my finger. It was an unforgettable night.

# Chapter 15

## Love, Intimacy, and Heartbreak

For the first time in my life, I was awake. I wanted to feel life, I wanted to be involved with the world, and I wanted to see everything. Nothing was ever going to pass me by again. This is what life was supposed to feel like: intense, complete, liberating, and magical. Julian awoke something in me, and I knew my life would never be the same.

My family was getting noticeably nervous about the seriousness of our relationship. They felt he had some sort spell over me. In their opinion, he was no good for me. They knew his type and said he was probably using me. My parents did everything they could to try to discourage me from going out with him. Finally, they forbade me to see him. I was upset. How could they be doing this to me when I was finally happy? I tried and tried to get them to understand, but they stood their ground. I got depressed and stopped talking to them. I couldn't face another day of pain and stress; it was as though I wasn't meant to be happy. Julian was miserable. He made daily attempts to try to contact me. Finally, after a week of calling and pleading with my parents, they told him that they would get the police involved if he didn't leave me alone.

My life was a struggle. *How can I go on now, when I know in my heart that there will be a lifetime of hardship and distress?* I was so overwhelmed with the thought of going back to the empty life I was living before Julian that I felt I couldn't go on. Life was hard. I had no fight in me, no energy to do it anymore. No matter how I tried, there were no words to convince my parents to trust me on this. I couldn't see him anymore, and I felt total despair.

In sheer desperation, I found a rope and tied a noose. This time I wouldn't fail. I put the rope in a bag and headed off to the old water tower, where I was going to hang myself. I got to the top of the hill and tied the rope to a thick branch, far enough from the cliff that my feet couldn't reach. I proceeded to slip the rope over my head, but I couldn't quite get it under my chin. My hands were shaking too much; I tied the rope too far and could barely reach. I tried for ten minutes until I was so exhausted I broke into tears and gave up. My entire body was shaking, and I sat against the tree trying to regain control. That was the moment I realized I wasn't meant to die. It was as though I were indestructible. No matter how hard I tried, I always failed.

I walked home, all the while trying to think of another way out of the desperation I felt. Everything seemed to be going out of control, and then I remembered the last visit I had with Rick's baby, Desiree. Julian and I took a drive to visit her that summer, and I could see my cousin was feeling guilty about the pain he caused our family by running off with Rick's wife. He was constantly trying to make things right in his own way. He told me that I could go to them with anything, and if I needed a place to stay, their door was always open. I decided that his words were especially instrumental in saving my life. I wasn't keen on living with Pam, but it was better than the overwhelming feeling of dread I was dealing with. I called him when I got home and took him up on his offer.

They tried to talk me out of leaving, but little did they know that my decision was based purely on survival.

My parents were upset about the whole thing, to say the least. They couldn't understand why I would want to live with Pam after everything she'd done to our family. I knew they only wanted what was best for me, but I couldn't cope with the pressure of complying with their wish that I break up with the man I loved so dearly. I knew in my heart that he was my soul mate.

Julian wasn't happy about the idea either, but then I confessed my feelings of despair and said I needed to put space between myself and everything else. He offered me his support and drove me to the bus station. Julian promised to call and visit me every other weekend. I promised to stay only long enough to get myself together. We kissed each other and said our good-byes. As the bus pulled out of the station, I already missed him terribly, but I also felt a wave of relief wash over me.

When I arrived, things were fine at first. I started school, and when I got home each day, I'd ask Pam if Julian had called. She'd look at me sympathetically and say, "Not yet."

Pam talked about the financial problems they were having and said they couldn't afford to have me stay unless I could help by paying room and board. I assured her I would get a part-time job as soon as I could. I didn't have the heart to ask her if I could make any long-distance calls. I wanted to call Julian badly, but I had to wait. Until then, I looked after the kids and did chores.

A few weeks later, we were sitting at the kitchen table having coffee. I'd had no luck finding a job and started to tell Pam I was thinking of going back home. "I've been looking for a job during my lunch breaks at school, and nobody's hiring. Even fast food joints aren't hiring."

She sat across from me, let out a long sigh, and said, "I wasn't going to say anything, but it looks like I don't have much choice right now. I've been talking to your mom, and although she wants you to come back, she says your dad is so upset he refuses to let you come back. Apparently, Julian got engaged to one of your friends … um, Alysia, I think is what she said. I'm so sorry you have to hear it this way, kid. Looks like he was just using you. You can't trust guys. They'll say anything to get you into their pants, you know."

I was frozen. I couldn't move. All I could do was cry, and Pam consoled me by telling me he was very charming and it could have happened to anyone; I just happened to be there when it suited him. I was crushed, yet everything she said seemed to make sense to me. He wasn't calling me; neither were my parents. I cried myself to sleep holding Julian's hockey shirt against me.

Every day was a nightmare. It seemed everywhere I looked I saw Julian. I longed for him. Alysia had never been a friend; she was more of an acquaintance I knew through my parents' friends. Pam supported me and offered me advice. "You need to put some closure to this mess by confronting him. Why don't you call him and give him a piece of your mind?"

"I don't want to do that."

"Why not? He's sleeping with your friend, and you're going to sit back and let it be? Listen, it's the only way you'll be able to get on with your life."

"Yeah, I guess you're right. What should I say?"

"Tell him you know about Alysia, and it's over. Short and sweet. Don't let him get the better of you."

I dialed his familiar number, and a part of me was hoping I'd hear the old spark in his voice. Then again, I was so angry at the lies, there was nothing left. The sound of his voice was bittersweet, but then I stood firm. "Julian? It's me. I know everything about Alysia, you know. How could you do that? It's over between us."

He just paused, and before I could hear his response, Pam hung up the phone and told me I did well and she was proud of me. I was angry at her for hanging up, but she justified it by saying she did it to protect me. He didn't try calling me back like I hoped, and she confirmed that I should be moving on like he was. Finally, she convinced me to sell my engagement ring. I wouldn't need it anymore; it was just a bad memory I should try to forget. I never felt as lonely as I did that day. I had absolutely nowhere to go. I wandered the streets for hours until I finally headed back, only to collapse into bed to cry myself to sleep. The rest of the week was a blur.

I decided I had to try to make amends with my dad, so I arranged to go home for a weekend visit. I left right after supper on the next bus out. I had just enough money to get home and back and buy a few meals. Pam had said the gas company was going to cut off their heat, so she'd borrowed the two hundred dollars I kept in the cookie jar.

I got home late that night and talked to my mom about everything Pam had told me. It all turned out to be lies. She'd had the nerve to manipulate me so that I would sell my ring, and I was angry at being played so very easily. On top of everything else she'd done to our family, she was even collecting my mother's baby bonus check which is a check that the federal government gives mothers in Canada for each child. The woman was horrible.

It was a relief to be home again. I wanted to see Julian, but after what I did to him, I didn't want to chance it by phone. I headed over to his house. I wanted to explain everything in person, and I wondered if there was any truth to the rumors of his engagement to Alysia. I decided not to expect too much. If all else failed, I was just going to apologize to him.

The October night had a crisp chill to it. I wore the beautiful cream-colored faux fur jacket I'd bought. I got off the bus a block before my stop so I could gather my thoughts and decide what I was going to say. I wondered if he would turn me away and tried to push those thoughts aside.

I had to stay positive and take that chance. The air smelled of burning firewood. I approached his door with fear and anticipation and knocked. There was no turning back. I heard a few steps, and the door opened. It was Julian; his eyes were full of both pain and relief. We just stared at each other. I didn't speak, and neither did he.

He stepped down and took me into his arms. With his lips against my neck, he whispered, "Never leave again. Never!"

I tried to tell him what happened, and he replied, "It's okay. I just want to hold you right now. We'll talk later. I never want to let you go."

We held each other and cried. Then we kissed as though we were reaching into each other's souls—lost souls found again. He went back inside to get a sweather, and we went for a walk in the cool night air. I told him everything about how Pam manipulated me with her half-truths and made me feel I had nowhere else to go. He said she told him I didn't want to speak to him whenever he called, and that she didn't know why. He wrote me letters that I never received.

He told me about Alysia. "She was on my doorstep just days after you left—to comfort me, as she put it. She tried to convince me that I should forget about you. Once she realized she wasn't getting anywhere, she suggested we drive up there to make you jealous. She suggested wearing a ring and telling you that we were engaged. She's crazy. She wouldn't leave me alone, and I tried to avoid her like the plague. Finally, I told her she wouldn't want a guy like me; I'd use her and drop her within the same week. She finally left me alone. I'd never have anything to do with her, Babe. I'm surprised you'd believe something like that."

What he said made sense. Alysia was one of the most dominant girls I knew. I didn't know what to think. "When I called you and asked about Alysia, you didn't deny anything. Pam was coaching me on what to say, and she hung up the phone. It killed me inside. But then she somehow convinced me to put everything behind me and get on with my life. That's when she convinced me to sell my ring to her neighbor's boyfriend. She must have arranged the whole thing. What a bitch! How could she do something so horrible? What would she gain from this?"

He smiled at me and said nothing could ever keep us apart. "I love you, and I'm never letting you out of my sight again."

> I adored him, but I didn't want to get overloaded again. This emotional roller-coaster ride had taken its toll on me. I needed to slow things down a notch so that I could have a sense of control until things settled down.

Besides, we didn't need anyone lecturing us anymore. We'd both had enough of everyone's opinions to last us a lifetime. I knew my parents were furious with him because of the rumors Pam and Alysia started, and it wouldn't be easy to convince them otherwise.

It was late when I got home. I had my first good night's sleep in four weeks and woke up late the next morning, refreshed and ready to face the day. I called Alysia to confront her, but part of me also needed to confirm the truth. I spoke to her with the pretense that it was over between Julian and I. She said, "It's a good thing you're done with him, Sophia. He told me he uses girls and leaves them." Those words were music to my ears. I was walking on air; Julian was telling me the truth. I thanked her and told her I had to go.

That day, I explained everything to my family. My mom believed me, but my dad was still skeptical about everything. He never trusted Pam, but he couldn't trust Julian, either. I knew the only thing that would change his opinion was time. That was okay for now. Julian and I enjoyed our time together, and each day brought us closer.

# Chapter 16

# It's a Girl

Four months had gone by since Julian and I had gotten back together. We spent almost every day together, and I soon discovered that I was pregnant. We were both very nervous, but mostly excited at the thought of our love growing inside of me. Julian was so happy the day we found out I was pregnant. He picked me up and swung me around, kissing my face. I couldn't believe how happy this man made me. Nobody could keep us apart now; our child was our bridge, joining us together for eternity. Somehow we knew, even at the tender age of sixteen, we would always be together.

We enjoyed every moment of our pregnancy. Julian talked and sang to our baby. He made sure I ate all the right things and never let me get upset. I left school shortly after I learned about my pregnancy, with the intention of returning soon. We found a little one-bedroom apartment in my seventh month of pregnancy and waited in anticipation for the arrival of our beautiful child. I read constantly about pregnancy when Julian was at work and quickly became somewhat of an expert on the subject.

September arrived; I was three weeks overdue and finally went into labor. Once the pains were more intense, we headed to the hospital for a long and difficult labor. Our sweet little girl was born. She was so beautiful and delicate that even the nurses said she was one of the prettiest babies they'd seen. Her birth was indescribable, and Julian cried at the very sight of her. "She's so beautiful, Babe. She has your lips!"

He was emotional. The nurse immediately placed our squalling baby in his arms, and she stopped crying. She looked up at him as he spoke to her; it was as though she knew he was the guy who greeted her and sang to her each day while she was comfortably resting in my womb. We talked about naming her Sara, which was the name of one of his ex-girlfriends. It had nothing to do with her; he just found it a beautiful name. His ex was exceptionally beautiful, with long, black, wavy hair and deep blue eyes. I never saw her, but I asked Julian about her many times. He said she was into some other guy, so it never worked out. I was so secure about his love for me that I agreed to name her Sara. The name suited her perfectly.

Raising our beautiful daughter was special. We packed her up and took her everywhere we went and included her in all that we did. She was an extension of our love, and I enjoyed watching Julian emerge into fatherhood. He helped me with her bottles, diaper changes, and feedings, and we just loved watching each milestone she crossed. He didn't miss a beat with her, and he was undeniably her favorite person. As soon as she heard his voice, she'd stop crying, look his way, and expect him to take her. I don't profess that it was easy to raise a child at such a young age, because it was the most difficult thing I ever had to do.

Without Julian's support, it would have been nearly impossible for me to manage on my own. Determination and pride were my driving force, and I did my best to give her the life she deserved.

It became a quest for me to raise her properly. Of course, I read incessantly about each stage of her development. This was due to my constant anxiety. The best way for me to calm my worries was to study, and that gave me the tools to deal with raising a child. I followed each stage of development, from potty training to separation anxiety, through library books. Julian supported and encouraged me, and together we did everything from shopping to cooking. We decided to hold off on getting married until we could afford a nice wedding.

# Chapter 17

# Coping through Desensitization

We lived in a beat-up apartment building when Sara was two years old. Julian ran into the living room one day. He picked me up and swung me around, shouting, "We won! Here, look for yourself!" He held out a lottery ticket. "We have five numbers—only one number and the bonus is missing!"

We were so excited all we could do to keep our wits was to rush through the house in search of the baby's hat and coat. I couldn't find her boots and laid the ticket on the kitchen table so I could quickly fetch them. As I was tying her hat, I noticed she was chewing on something. To my horror, it was the lottery ticket, chewed up into a tight little pink ball. It was totally destroyed, and to make matters worse, Sara never chewed paper before or after that unfortunate day. We never did find out how much money we won and lost in those glorious fifteen minutes of freedom, nor did we want to know. It could have been anywhere from five thousand to fifty thousand or more. Whatever it was, we needed it in a bad way, and I screwed it up by being careless and absentminded. I can't help thinking back on Julian's reaction. He was disappointed, but he tried to cheer me up by reasoning that we probably weren't meant to have it and that it was okay. We look back on this and laugh, but that week was a solemn one.

I knew I had to distract myself, so I bought a romance novel. Reading was a passion for me. It was and still is a means of escaping to another land. My favorite books were historical romance novels, and I read self-help books while Sara slept. Every so often, I'd stay up at night and read an entire book in six hours or less.

Meanwhile, I was secretly harboring insecurities about Julian's ex, Sara. I decided it was silly and that I should make it a personal goal to lose the weight I'd gained during my pregnancy, but for some reason the thoughts I had still nagged at me. It started innocently enough; I was determined to look great just to make sure Julian wouldn't regret his decision to be with me. The pounds came off rather easily, and I would continue to lose a little more until I had lost over thirty pounds. I looked anorexic, and everyone kept telling me to stop losing weight. I was convinced I looked great and that people were just jealous. One day, I had a good look at myself in a full-length mirror and realized my breasts had almost disappeared. I was absolutely horrified. I was also confused about how I'd never realized it until that day. I began to slowly gain weight until I reached a healthy 114 pounds. I was very satisfied with how I looked. Everything was in all the right places, and my confidence was restored.

I decided to go back to school, since my first job experience as a waitress was a complete disaster. I couldn't remember which table ordered what because I didn't remember faces, and I spilled drinks on people. After about six weeks, I admitted everything to the manager. I said I had to leave before her business suffered too much. Customers were walking out because of me. She was very nice and told me I should give myself a chance to get the hang of it. I thought she was nuts and insisted that I would return to school. She wished me luck, and within two months I was accepted in an adult training program at a local college. My mother offered to watch Sara and Julian worked for his father's contruction company.

My first day was both exciting and frightening, but I decided to push myself to try to experience everything. I went to the gym on my lunch hour. I lost track of the time and was late for class, so I rushed into the dressing room and into the showers, only to notice a chubby woman with short, curly hair showering with her back to me. As she turned to face me, I realized she was a he. I frantically tried to pull open the door, which turned out to be jammed. I tried the door next to it, only to find another guy sitting on the toilet. I pushed open the first door to finally escape to the hall, then to the ladies' dressing room, where I quickly dressed and rushed off to class. I was angry with myself. Because of my bad sense of direction, I had run into the men's dressing room and now I was late for class. Every time I saw that fellow in the hall, he looked down in humiliation and I laughed to myself.

I studied relentlessly and was pleasantly surprised to discover how well I absorbed the information. I celebrated each A I earned, which brought me closer to my goal. Within eight months, I was accepted in a general business administration program.

This is when I discovered learning through association. I did this by visualizing my thoughts into pictures. I was better able to learn on my own this way, rather than trying to decode and follow the lessons taught by a teacher.

The most difficult part of my day was walking through the cafeteria at lunchtime, where I was greeted with whistles and comments until I thought my legs would buckle. I avoided the cafeteria as much as I could and mostly kept to myself. Eventually, I did make a few friends, which made life in the cafeteria a lot more bearable.

The two friends I made were Jake and Shawn. They were quite a bit older than I was and treated me with respect. Julian and I started hanging out with them and their wives, Lynn and Nadine. They were especially nice and loved to have a laugh. They all loved Julian's sense of humor, and we would hang out together as couples. We went to clubs together or hung out at each other's apartments, and I quickly became close friends with Nadine. She was my friend and confidante. Every week, we had coffee together or went shopping. Nadine talked constantly, which made the one-on-one easy, but I often wondered if she enjoyed my company as much as I did hers. It might sound strange, but I used to try to focus on something I knew she would be interested in before knocking at her door. This method helped me feel secure about initializing the topic of conversation.

I really enjoyed college, but it made me painfully aware of how uncomfortable my shyness made me, and I was determined to try to change it. I began my quest to desensitize myself after I saw a live show on the power of suggestion.

Later that week, Julian and I were at a nightclub when the DJ announced they were having a bikini contest and needed one more contestant. This was it; the chance to overcome my shyness was facing me now. Julian gave me the encouragement to walk over and sign up. We headed home to get my bikini and heels. Before I knew it, I was touching up my makeup and getting ready to step onto the stage with two other girls. I was so nervous that my legs were like rubber. I walked about the stage and mimicked the other two girls as I danced. The only way I could get through it was to imagine I was alone. The crowd voted with loud cheers and, to my surprise, I placed first in the contest. I won a spot in the finals, fifty dollars, and a bottle of wine. I was proud of myself. I'd pulled it off, far exceeding any expectations I'd had an hour before. I danced on air for four weeks until my next competition. Something about the anticipation really screwed me up, though. It was horrible; I froze, forgot my own age, and placed third. To say I was disappointed would be an understatement. I felt betrayed by my own mind. Unfortunately, it really affected me. I was so crushed that I had a seizure the next morning in math class. I took a few days off to recuperate and to put some distance between myself and the week's events.

I didn't give up, however. I found myself singing on stage at a karaoke bar a short while after. It was extremely nerve-wracking, but I got used to it, and it helped me through a multitude of situations. It also showed me that pushing myself a little was one of the best ways to develop my social skills.

I buried myself in my studies and eventually graduated third in my class. I was proud, but I felt I could have done better. I received a C minus in my co-op class due to the fact that the teacher claimed I didn't seem interested in participating. I tried to tell her it was just shyness and that it takes me a long time to get comfortable, but she wouldn't budge. I knew I had big hurdles to overcome, and my biggest fear was the inevitable transition I had to make to the work force. I didn't know how I was going to do it. Each time I spoke to a prospective employer, I was so nervous my voice shook and I lost my train of thought.

I started creating scripts for myself and practicing them. Eventually, I was hired as a receptionist with a temporary agency. I became consumed with learning everything I could. My goal was to become indispensable .

Although I had trouble remembering details, I did all I could to try to master the skills of my position. The problem was that the dedication I displayed was noticed by co-workers competing for full-time jobs, and I was often subjected to jealousy and sabotage. I got into trouble for stupid things like forgetting to turn off my computer at the end of the day. They'd run to my boss with anything I did wrong. By the time five o'clock came, I was exhausted. It seemed I spent most of my day double-checking everything I did and staying on top of my duties. My new goal was to avoid getting caught with my guard down, and I counted the days to the end of the contract so that I could start new again.

I smiled and tried to say all the right things. People always seemed to ask me, "Are you for real? Don't you ever get upset? What's your secret?"

My secret? My very existence was a secret.

That was when I realized that no one ever really understood my essence. No one except my family, and even they would never know the very core of my true self. Julian often wondered why I treated him and Sara differently than I treated others. He said I was much nicer to others than I was to them. I was diplomatic when it came to anyone else. Julian and I often argued about this. He said I was going about it all wrong. I didn't know how else to relate. I needed to be myself, and his perception of the whole situation really seemed to bother him.

# Chapter 18

# The Wedding

There were always gatherings with Julian's family, and I was painfully shy around them. His parents were the kindest people you could meet, and his three brothers and sister were energetic, witty, and intelligent. Getting a word in was always a bit of a challenge, and I'm still grateful for that, because the pressures of filling uncomfortable silences were kept to a minimum. I very much enjoyed their company, but keeping track of conversations was difficult. I did much better one-on-one, but the bulk of our conversations involved the kids, and small talk was an effort for me. It seemed to me that the only way I was able to get reasonably comfortable around Julian's family was to have a few drinks. It helped me to relax and get over the awkward shyness I felt. Although I enjoyed their company, at times I found it to be emotionally exhausting, especially if it was a weekend event with a lot of people.

We spent most of our summer weekends at the cottage. It was like strolling into the past, the birthplace of our love. Julian's dad, Tom, built a sleep camp where we stayed. He was one of the most generous people I knew, and he was constantly kidding around. Until I got used to it, I was never sure whether I should laugh or be serious around him. Julian's mother, Joceline, was a delicate yet trendy woman with a young heart. You could count on her to try anything, not only once, but over and over.

Having both our parents' cottages so close to each other was really convenient. The fact that I was able to walk a few yards over to my parents' cottage was a bonus. It gave me a way out if things got uncomfortable for me. Nonetheless, it took me at least three years to find a comfort level around Julian's parents, and almost twenty years for me to stop addressing them by Mrs and Mrs. Summers and to start addressing them by their first names.

Julian's three brothers and sister were fun to be around. Although they each had their own unique personalities, I saw part of Julian in each of them, especially the crazy sense of humor they shared. Julian's oldest brother, Danny, the most perplexingly intense member of the family, initiated many of our activities, from swimming to boating, and even parasailing—that's a story for another book. A weekend with Julian's family was always filled with laughter and excitement.

> Their contrast to my serious world was exactly what I needed all these years, and I looked forward to our weekends.

Sara was three years old when we started planning our wedding. It was my new obsession, and I planned it completely and flawlessly. By then I'd fallen in love with Julian's family and was able to relax around them more and more, especially when we planned the wedding. My sister Natalie stood as my maid of honor, with Julian's younger brother Alex as best man. Alex was best known for his caring personality and playful, flirtatious ways; he was funny in a klutzy sort of way, and dedicated to his little family. Julian's sister Jennifer was my bridesmaid, and her husband, Brian, was best man. Jennifer still doesn't know it, but she's been a strong influence in my life. She's fun-loving, easy to talk to, and full of energy.

> I've appreciated her confidence and wit over the years and found myself modeling many of her social skills.

Brian admired her from afar, and the two of them playfully teased each other. Brian and Alex welcomed me into the family from day one. They caught on to my shyness and tried their best to make me feel comfortable. They were enthusiastic about the wedding, and it was extremely exciting.

I eagerly embarked on this journey, which would lead us to be joined as husband and wife. Each morning I woke up to the thoughts of our wedding, and I fell asleep with those same thoughts, leaving me confused and with mixed emotions. I questioned the idea of this obsession and wondered if I was losing sight of the significance of the day. Was I getting married for the sheer pleasure of planning it? Don't get me wrong. I loved Julian without a doubt, and I knew our day would be special. I just couldn't figure out why I was so fixated on one day.

The big moment finally arrived, and my parents walked me down the aisle. My knees felt weak as I walked by our families and relatives. Julian's eight-year-old brother, Will, who was extremely shy, played the wedding march beautifully on the organ. That kid made me proud. The church was full, and I could hear comments coming from either side of me saying that I looked like a porcelain doll. I glanced up to see Julian waiting for me. He wore a white tuxedo and a look of tenderness and anticipation. He was beautiful, and all I wanted at that moment was to be in his arms. I didn't hear much of what the priest said during the ceremony. I just wanted him to hurry up and marry us so we could be in each other's arms. I cried as we said our vows. When we were pronounced husband and wife, we kissed and held each other so long the priest actually tapped us on the shoulders to prompt us to move apart. It was the most beautiful feeling to finally be united as soul mates. We were only aware of each other. We started down the aisle together to be greeted by camera flashes and emotional, tearful family members and friends. The reception was superb, the music was great, and everyone enjoyed each other tremendously. I was glad when the music started because it helped to me relax as I mingled, which was uncomfortable unless I had someone with me.

We drove to Ottawa for our honeymoon and lived gloriously in the moment, as though we were the only two people in existence.

# Chapter 19

# It's a Boy

Immediately after our honeymoon, I began to work for various companies on temporary assignments. My contracts ranged anywhere from monthly to yearly. It was difficult at first, but I got used to the changes.

I fed on Julian's encouragement and the pride he displayed when I told him of my accomplishments. I worked as a receptionist and was consumed with learning everything I could. I eventually became a model employee.

In a way, I was happy with changing jobs because I didn't have to get to the personal level, where they would know the real me. Mimicking other personalities was my way of coping. At the same time, it was extremely exhausting to keep up. I spent my time smiling and trying to say all the right things. Nobody knew what I felt inside: guarded and insecure. Yet I looked confident and sometimes even aloof. Every thought that crossed my mind was, in one way or another, second-guessing my every move. I thought everything out before speaking. Once I had the right words, if the conversation shifted too often, I remained quiet. As soon as I was comfortable enough, I thought a little less and talked a little more. Sometimes the timing was off or the words came out wrong. It was worse if I started talking and then drew a blank, frantically searching for the word I wanted to say. Living on the sidelines was comfortable for me; nevertheless, a deep-seated part of me wished I was in the game. Some considered me forgetful; others considered me quirky and whimsical.

I quickly gained the reputation of being sweet and funny. I learned how to use this to my advantage. Before long, I had mastered the art of charming my way into job interviews and getting hired rather quickly using my acting skills.

I had an interview on a Friday morning. The position was to start on Monday. It was quite empowering to watch the interviewers hang on my every word, yet it was alien to me. I exaggerated my computer skills, knowing quite well that I would have to cram like mad over the weekend to master the skills I so blatantly lied about. I was glad to be hired on the spot, yet a small part of me regretted having to live up to the pressures and expectations I'd placed upon myself just moments before.

I couldn't believe I'd landed a great job at a university. It meant free education for my family, and I was excited. Handling the switchboard along with the heavy workload I was given was stressing me out, but I reasoned that each day would be easier. I had trouble keeping up, and it didn't help matters that I refused to ask for help.

My computer skills were lacking, but I did my best to figure everything out on my own. It was stressful, but I kept my head above water, got home exhausted, and started it all again the next day.

A few months later, my boss commented that he thought he'd hired someone else. He meant to say I was not the same person that he saw at the interview, and he asked me if I had problems at home. That was quite upsetting. I felt like he could see right through me, which made me even more self-conscious. I wished it was as simple as that. How could I explain my changing personality except to say I was going through a stressful time at the moment? My dreams came crashing down the day my boss called me into his office and explained that he had to let me go because he'd made a mistake. He said I did well in the interview, yet I didn't have the experience needed for this position.

No words can even begin to describe the devastation and shame I felt. I wondered how I was going to tell Julian. My last day came around; I packed my things and walked to my car feeling defeated. Two weeks later, my old boss called to offer me my job back because my replacement didn't work out. I graciously declined, of course. He had the nerve to let me go, then to call me back to replace my replacement? I was both annoyed and satisfied. There was no way I was going back to face anyone there or answer any of their questions.

Besides, I was working with the temporary agency and, so far, things were going as well as can be expected. I still felt depressed and especially inadequate; I'd had a seizure my first week and ended up being let go. I took a few months off, and my relationship with Julian began to suffer. He was working at an entry-level position in sales, and money was really tight. We had to move into a smaller apartment to make ends meet.

Sara was already six years old. We'd talked about having another baby for a few years now, but everything was falling apart. Julian kept insisting it was the wrong time. I knew he was right, but at the rate we were going, it would never be the right time, and didn't want Sara to grow up an only child. Sara kept asking for a baby sister or brother to play with, and we could see how lonely she was. She played hide and seek with Ginger, our cat. She'd hide for what seemed an eternity, never to be found. We'd hear her calling Ginger, and as soon as the cat got anywhere near her, she'd dart out of her hiding place to her safe place. It was cute and sad at the same time. I needed a break from all the disappointments we experienced, and getting pregnant had become somewhat of an obsession with me.

I started negotiating a commitment from Julian, and we came to a mutual understanding, or so I thought. We would start trying as soon as I was settled into a full-time job, as we'd planned before.

I knew he was apprehensive but assured him all would go well this time. Nothing was happening, but sure enough, four months later, I was pregnant and thrilled. My job as a data entry clerk was easy. There was no pressure and the people were nice. We were on our way to completing our little family, and I was doing well for a change.

A few months later, things with Julian seemed different. He was unusually quiet and withdrawn. He insisted there was nothing wrong, but I later found out business was slow and he was dipping into our credit cards for food and rent. He kept his frustrations bottled up until one day when he lashed out at me with a year's worth of resentment. I felt as though my insides were being pulled out of me. How could I be so blind that I didn't see how the pressure of providing for us was affecting him? If we weren't arguing, there was an uncomfortable silence.

Our lives had become so complicated I cried almost every day. I realized that I'd forced my plans on him when he wasn't ready. Stress was really taking its toll, and I had a seizure a few weeks later. I woke up to Julian leaning over me in our bedroom. He took me to the emergency room, where the doctor reassured me that the ultrasound showed no signs of trauma to the baby. From that point on, I was careful not to get upset. The anger and frustration had suddenly left Julian's face, replaced by the nurturing love and appreciation that had been buried for so long. The bond we once had resurfaced.

Our beautiful son, Josh, was born in May, and we were elated. He was a strong and solid boy and stopped crying the very moment he felt my touch. Julian leaned over the baby and kissed his brand-new little forehead. He turned to me and stroked my hair. With a look of quiet contentment, he thanked me for giving him such a beautiful son. I was glad to have my boy and imagined watching him grow into the likeness of the man I loved.

Julian went to work for his father as a carpenter. It's not what he imagined for himself, but the important thing was that we were managing our finances. I could see his worries drift away. He said he could always find a better opportunity once our lives were stable. The hard times we experienced were coming to an end, and it was nice to hear laughter in the house again.

Josh was a good baby. He was quiet and only fussed for feedings or his soother. Otherwise, he pretty much kept himself amused. We took every opportunity to spend quality time with Sara after school or on weekends by taking her to the park or playing a game together at home as the baby slept.

When Sara was at school, I spent quality time with Josh. He was fascinated with our ceiling fan; he appeared to be trying to figure out what made it spin. He loved his spinning top and could have easily watched it for hours. His spinning fascination continued when he learned to spin random objects, like spoons, the hairbrush, and, eventually, the wheels on his toy cars.

We were taken by surprise when at eight months Josh clearly repeated the words, "Hi, Dad," in the exact same tone Julian used each morning when he greeted him. Josh enjoyed being by himself, and as he got older he preferred to drink his bottle propped up with a blanket while he lay on his back. He often played with his toys in peculiar ways. If he wasn't spinning the wheels on his cars, he lined them up like a train or a parking lot. He tended to place the things he played with in some sort of sequence and got very upset if it was disturbed in any way. We had to be careful not to put his toys away unless he interrupted the sequence himself.

Sara was a good sister to Josh; however, she complained that having a baby wasn't quite what she expected. She thought it would be fun and they would play together. She didn't have an active role or much of a relationship yet with the baby. I guess I expected it to come more naturally, but it didn't seem to. Josh didn't notice his sister, and she seemed to feel excluded. As the months progressed, she started showing signs of insecurity. We tried to do all the right things for her, but it was never enough. Raising our children properly was a source of satisfaction and pride for us, but eventually it became more of an obsession and a source of intense stress for me. If Sara misbehaved more than usual, I felt I was failing her, and I became someone I hated. I would literally freak out if circumstances were out of my control, which was often. I fought with Sara and Julian, and he urged me to get help. Out in public, nobody knew. I hid everything so well that I even frightened myself. The emotions I experienced ran deep until the anxiety manifested itself in sheer panic. With the feeling of panic came a loss of control. It was such a gradual process that I didn't realize what was coming over me. Sara, of course, met my efforts with resentment. It was too late. She no longer trusted me, and now she resented her baby brother.

I knew something was wrong; Julian and I argued to the point of almost ending our relationship way too often.

I tried to read up on anything I could find to help me deal with this, but nothing matched what we were going through. I started seeing the doctor so we could get counseling, but the doctor insisted I could talk to him. The waiting lists were long where we lived, and he felt the sooner I dealt with these issues, the better.

I told him I felt suicidal, but not to the point of attempting it. Talking to him helped somewhat, but it wasn't nearly enough. Nothing changed in the way I handled my anxieties toward raising my kids, and eventually I resorted to slapping Sara when nothing else worked. I made sure not to slap her hard, but at the same time I compensated by yelling to scare her into learning her lesson. By the time Sara was ten and Josh was two, I had damaged my relationship with them and hated myself for not having more self-control. Julian and the kids helplessly watched me have a major emotional breakdown. The strangest thing was that the more he tried to convince me that I needed help, the more I resisted. At this point, I didn't believe him. Although I found it difficult to hold myself together, I felt everyone was overreacting about the whole situation. I thought I was depressed and everyone was making life harder for me.

I was finding it difficult to hold everything together, so I decided to stay at home with Josh for a while. The assignment I was working on with a temp agency was coming to an end, and we were doing much better financially. I was able to relax and put things into perspective. I did the best I could to repair the damage to my family.

I sat down with Sara to explain to her how I was under tremendous pressure and just wanted to teach her right from wrong. I apologized for my behavior and reassured her that I loved her more than she could imagine and that I never meant to hurt her.

She cried, and we held each other for a long time. Things between us improved, and I could see her insecurities slowly fade.

I treasured my much-needed time at home with Josh, and things were better for me emotionally. I needed this time to breathe. I noticed his thirst for knowledge when I read to him. He pointed to letters that he wanted me to say, and he would repeat them. He continued to do so by chasing after anyone who could read off the letters to him. By the time he was two years old, he could read all the letters of the alphabet in uppercase and lowercase, in random order, in both French and English. He also mastered his numbers from one to ten. We were all amazed and happy, and we nurtured his abilities every chance we got.

I spent over a year with him. Then I decided it was time for me to return to school so that I could have a stable career. Josh attended the college daycare, and his teachers marveled at his skills. He could remember everybody's names and was exceptionally skilled at putting together puzzles. But not long after he started daycare, he stopped talking completely and experienced extreme separation anxiety. I dreaded mornings and often cried after leaving him. He threw huge fits, and I sensed something was wrong in the way he looked at me. He had a look of sheer panic on his face, and it wasn't long until he knew the way there and screamed when I made that dreaded left-hand turn leading towards the daycare.

My first inclination was to think something was wrong at the daycare, and initially I was suspicious about the treatment he received. I spoke to the supervisor about my concerns, and she convinced me it was separation anxiety and time would rectify everything.

When months had passed and he still wasn't talking, the daycare provided support. Eventually, a series of tests revealed a developmental disability, which invariably led to a diagnosis of high-functioning autism. Josh's symptoms were first noticed by his daycare when he was a toddler. They referred us to a child psychologist, who closely studied Josh for over six months.

I have always been especially protective of Josh due to the fact that I sensed his vulnerability, but now I realize and appreciate the crucial importance of preparing him for life's challenges by offering him the right tools. Although he's made great strides, there is always more to overcome with each stage of development.

It was upon Josh's diagnosis that my suspicions about my own well-being really originated. The psychologist described everything along the lines of my own difficulties, especially when he pointed out some of Josh's symptoms. I remember thinking, *That's not so abnormal; it sounds like he's just painfully shy and quiet, just like I was as a child.* My son had little interest in other children and preferred to play by himself by placing his toys in a line or spinning the wheels of his cars for hours at a time. Needless to say, it came as a shock to hear the following words that led to our son's eventual diagnosis. We just couldn't believe that there could be something wrong with Josh. We considered him a gifted child and had high hopes for his future.

I was sitting at the kitchen table with the social worker, Deborah, when she explained the results of the tests he had taken. "Josh is displaying signs of PDD NOS, which is a pervasive developmental disorder not otherwise specified, which is on a continuum of the autism spectrum." She went on to explain that it was a developmental disorder with a tendency to withdraw from social situations due to difficulties associated in decoding social cues.

I sat there in disbelief. I never noticed anything drastic about Josh that would indicate a problem. Deborah was still talking to me, but I felt numb and could only hear the distant droning of her voice. All I could do was repeat the words "disorder" and "syndrome" in my mind until I found the words to ask, "Is Josh disabled?"

She replied, "Yes, he is. However, he needs to undergo further tests in order to determine where he fits on the autism spectrum. There are varying degrees. The good news is that he fits into the high-functioning autism spectrum of the disorder. As long as he gets help early, we can expect a better prognosis for his future."

"Will he be able to work and live independently as an adult?"

"It's still too early to know; only time will tell. Many people do go on to lead normal, independent lives. But again, it depends on many factors. Where he fits on the autism spectrum and early intervention often determines a positive prognosis."

Julian was at work; Deborah asked me if there was someone I could call for support. She gave me reading material and names and numbers for support groups, and said I could call her if I needed to talk. I felt cheated and upset. All I knew was that our sweet boy had to endure a life of injustice and he'd done nothing to deserve it. I had so many questions, and nothing had prepared me for what we were about to face. We were shocked and confused; we mourned the loss of our son's future. Initially, Julian's reaction was disbelief. He said they didn't know what they were talking about. I knew in my heart they were right and hated them for that. All the facts were there, and Julian seemed to resent my repeated attempts to explaining the logic of it to him. He changed the subject every time I brought it up, and I felt very alone in my quest to help our son.

> I absorbed as much information as possible in order to provide him with all the advantages I could. At least we knew what it was. We'd found out early, and we could do everything possible to help him.

The pediatrician also said that if we got an early start, Josh would have a better chance at a normal life. With time, Julian accepted it, but still insisted it wasn't as serious as we previously anticipated. He gave me a little thread of hope to hang on to. Suddenly, things didn't appear as grim as before.

We worked continuously with his therapist, Deborah. She was a remarkably caring woman and was one of the few people able to reach Josh. She patiently worked with him and taught us how to handle situations as they came up. His weekly therapy consisted of behavior modification, special education, social skills therapy, occupational therapy and speech therapy three times a week. Josh was formally diagnosed with Asperger's syndrome. The trials we faced had been extremely difficult for him and our family, but the sessions helped tremendously.

Unfortunately, the services were cut off when he reached six years old. We did the best we could to continue the work Deborah had taught us.

> I started to relax a bit and enjoy him. More than anything, I felt he needed to have fun so that he could relax. It wasn't long before we learned how to make him feel safe by taking him out of situations that were too stimulating for him. We left birthday parties early just to provide him with relief.

Each party and get-together got easier with time, and he was able to stay for longer periods. He still wasn't talking, and the therapist suggested we stick to one language. She explained that in his case it was more important to master one language than to have difficulties and delays in two languages. This was the best suggestion by far.

He was three years old when we began the transition to English only, and within days something fabulous happened. I will never forget that moment. I was in his bedroom, washing away the scribbles he'd made moments before on his closet door. I felt him watching me, and as I turned around to look at him, he stood with a look of concern on his face. I could see his round little belly heave up and down. He took a few deep breaths and in a shaky tone of voice he said, "Wh ... what ... happened?"

I dropped my washcloth. He hadn't spoken in months, and his words were music to my ears. For the first time in months, my son was back. I immediately hugged him and said, "Oh, Josh, you happened!" I giggled and said, "Look! You're talking, Josh! What a good boy. Mommy knew you could do it! I love you so much."

He looked like he was more aware of me and his surroundings. It was like he could really see the things around him, rather than looking through the room. He was quite pleased with himself. I took him to see his sister to share the good news, and we celebrated his success again when his dad arrived. From that day forward, his vocabulary flourished and he was proudly speaking three-word sentences. There was room for him in the English section of his daycare, which limited the stress to a comfortable degree. And since it was still summertime, he wouldn't have to start school until the fall.

Things were looking up. We felt more positive than we had in years.

We continued to develop his coping skills by telling him what to expect at least ten minutes beforehand. If we took a different route on our way somewhere, he had a screaming fit unless we told him in advance we had to make a stop. That way, he could get used to the idea. He hated surprises. As long as he was warned ahead of time, there was much less resistance on his part.

That summer was sort of funny. He was fascinated with bugs and loved to eat them. There was nothing we could do to prevent this except to watch him like a hawk. We continuously chased him around, trying to get him to release his tightfisted grasp on bugs, ants, and even dragonflies before he succeeded in shoving them into his mouth. He used to rub his belly and say, "Mmm, good!" I was glad when that phase ended.

Dinnertime was difficult, as he was extremely fussy. His diet consisted of only half a dozen meals. We couldn't get him to try new foods, but he ate various types of bugs—I still don't understand that one. He'd get upset if the food on his plate touched, and he would refuse to eat it. As long as we made sure everything on his plate was appealingly arranged, he was fine. I do understand why he doesn't like his food to touch. It's because when the flavors of two foods blend together, the end result is a random, unexpected taste.

# Chapter 20

# Career Breakthrough

Due to the high demand in our area, I decided to enroll in a dental assistant program. It was a one-year program, and I was able to get funding. I did extremely well, and I especially liked my science and anatomy classes. However, I didn't do well with my hand-eye coordination. I knew in my gut this would be a challenge. The closer it came to graduation, the more anxiety I felt. My clumsiness was a nagging reminder of the inevitable. I resented the guidance counselor for helping me make such a stupid career choice. I could have done that on my own.

Just when we thought our lives were getting back to normal, the market for dental assistants became saturated. By the time I graduated, I discovered the majority of dentists in our city were right-handed. When I did my co-op, I realized being left-handed was my worst drawback. I was totally clumsy, and I both crowded and annoyed the dentist. After much searching, I finally found a dentist who was left-handed and needed an assistant. I was hired on a Wednesday by Dr. Jenson, a sweet man in his sixties who was easygoing and kind. He said he appreciated my lack of experience and explained it was better to train and mold an employee if there were no old habits to break. I was to start on Monday, and I rushed home to share the news with Julian. We celebrated the promise of a bright future that weekend, and life was good. The fear and insecurity that plagued me before were gone, and I knew this was the place for me.

We were watching the news over the weekend when a drowning was reported. To my disbelief, they announced that a Dr. Jenson had drowned on a fishing trip early that morning. Julian and I looked at each other in shock. How could this be? Did I attract chaos or something? He was the only left-handed dentist I knew of in the city, and he'd died that morning. I know I should have felt for him and his family, but I was just numb. I should have sent flowers or a card, but I was too self-absorbed. All I could think of was my own loss.

I decided to forget about finding a job in my field and started looking for an office job. Within a week, I started working for a local floor covering company as a bookkeeper. Russ was the owner, and he took me under his wing. He was in his early seventies. He had a strong presence and a demeanor quite similar to that of Dean Martin. He spent each day training me in his own unique style.

His logic was, if you perform every step of the job in the very same sequence, the consistency will become a habit and errors will be less likely. It will become a natural extension of you, and the motions will be automatic.

He thought in a way I could relate to, and he was right about his theory. I've adopted his style as my own in many things.

The girls in the office were very jealous of the rapport I had with Russ and made every attempt they could to point out any errors I made along the way. It wasn't long before Russ realized what they were doing. He was livid and ordered them to pipe down. He protected me like I was his own child. Everything was great until he left for his annual trip to Florida. His two sons took over, and Russ wouldn't be back for four months. The two girls in the office took every opportunity to make my life there a living hell in the hopes that I would quit. They added to my determination to stick it out. I worked as hard and as fast as I could. Before too long, Russ's son Larry called them off. He said he was tired of hearing their gossip and bickering.

I told Russ and his son Steve that I wanted to stop sitting on the sidelines. It was time for me to get into the game.

> By the time I entered my second year there, I was feeling much braver. I continued my quest to get over my shyness by forcing myself to participate in social situations. I eventually earned a promotion to sales.

This was an enormous step for me, but I forced myself into it every day. Once I got over the awkward stage of greeting customers, my acting skills came into play. I eventually became one of Russ's most skilled sales reps. It was absolutely necessary for me to ensure that customers received the knowledge needed to make an educated decision, and I pointed out the best value for their dollar. I loved role-playing in every aspect of my life and was surprisingly efficient at convincing customers when it came to quality. Customers adored me, and I marveled at the thought that they knew nothing about who I really was. Russ considered me his protégé. Eventually, we got into deep discussions about business, philosophy, and life. He was one of the most interesting people I have ever known, and we genuinely enjoyed each other's company.

# Chapter 21

# Thinking in Pictures

I read the book *Thinking in Pictures* by Temple Grandin. I was amazed at my familiarity with the way she could take a mental snapshot of a particular scene and file it away. This really hit home for me because, until then, I assumed everyone naturally did this. That's exactly how Josh and I absorb information.

> We can retrieve any memory this way. By reviewing the snapshot, other information associated with that memory surfaces in a complete picture, along with the emotions.

Personally, from the time I was two and a half, I've always had the good fortune of being able to access memories with amazing accuracy. Until I realized that others didn't share this ability, I used to get frustrated with people if they couldn't even recall what I was reminiscing about in detail.

Josh is especially skilled at playing video games. He can play the game once and remember it like a map etched in his memory. Josh never really had to study in school, and math and languages always came quite easily to him. He would just read the material a few times and repeat much of it word-for-word when we quizzed him. His teacher was surprised at how he could do math problems without writing them down on paper. His response to her was, "I think it's pretty useless to write it down when you already know the answer." His biggest challenge was completing assignments. He either misplaced them or forgot to finish his work. On many occasions he'd scramble at the last minute trying to finish it off, which was visibly stressful for him. The last thing he wanted was to be singled out in class.

We explored various ways of helping him, including therapy and anxiety medication. At one point, we tried vitamin B therapy. The vitamins helped his concentration and made him healthier but didn't seem to help with many of the features associated with the syndrome. There were some improvements from the therapy sessions and medication he received, but it didn't help him in terms of dealing with social situations. Something was still missing.

When Josh was eight, we bought him a computer. He was glued to it from day one, playing games and searching the Web for anything that interested him. It was quite remarkable to see how quickly he was able to execute the most complex commands without being taught. He'd found his niche, and he was clearly happier. We tried to broaden his interests, but it was difficult. We tried to place time restraints on him, but that wasn't easy, either.

We discovered purely by chance that reasoning with him was the best course of action—there was logic behind it. We sat with him one day and said we had something very important to discuss and needed his feedback. We explained that if he did too much of one thing and ignored everything else, he would someday look back on his childhood with regret.

He understood at once, and we came to a mutual agreement. After that, our efforts met with less resistance.

Josh made many attempts at making new friends, but he wasn't sure how to go about it. We made that discovery when he commented that our neighborhood was filled with old people. He went door-to-door asking if there were kids he could play with and was turned down with comments that he was sweet, but their kids were grown up and gone. He succeeded in making a few neighborhood friends who all loved playing video games. Josh was an exceptionally skilled player. His friends couldn't keep up with him, and sometimes got discouraged and ran home. He topped everyone's scores, including his sister's friends. He rode his bike with his friends, and they played with their remote control cars and had water fights like all kids.

We were pleased with his progress. He was doing great, and I could see his confidence soar as his friends accepted his little eccentricities. Actually, they seemed to enjoy them. He used his imagination in play, and they would reenact parts of video games. Although it appeared odd at times, they seemed to have fun. Josh could have played the same game for hours. He didn't catch on to the social cues to change to another game. I used to prompt him to change their play with suggestions. I later explained to him that other kids didn't have the attention span to play the same game for too long. Periodically, with wide-eyed innocence, he would ask his friends if they still wanted to play their game.

# Chapter 22

## Into Death's Eyes

It was around this time that I gradually became interested in religion. I hoped to get some type of emotional relief by searching for answers in the bible. Religion made me feel as though I had some level of control, but it had the exact opposite effect on Julian. My outlook on life had changed. For instance, I only made love, and sex didn't fit into the equation. This freed me of the guilt I felt, for I was compelled to think that making love was beautiful and having sex was dirty. You could have sex while making love, but in my mind, having sex without making love was wrong. This thought process was probably due to various factors: upbringing, religious beliefs, and a naïve misunderstanding of my mother's words of wisdom. In any case, my belief was strong.

I was so hung up on religion in this phase of my life that I compared it to looking through a good pair of glasses. It all seemed clear to me. I couldn't think of anything else, and I felt an amazing euphoria. It consumed every part of my life and annoyed everyone else. I thought Julian would follow suit, but it gradually affected our relationship.

We lived next to an elderly couple, Tom and Martha. He was a war veteran, and very fit for his eighty-two years. Martha was the woman he loved to take care of, and she proudly commented about how good he was to her. You could always see them working in their backyard. He had the most interesting stories about his days at war, and Martha endearingly watched him as he retold tales she must have heard many times before.

I was sweeping our driveway one day when Tom said, "I'm going to have to cut down this old tree. It's rotting, and the branches are starting to fall in your driveway."

"Don't worry about it, Tom. Julian has a chainsaw, and he can do it for you when he gets back from work."

But Tom was a stubborn old guy. No matter what I said, he was going to cut that tree down himself. Before you knew it, he had the ladder up against the tree. I couldn't stay out there. I watched him from my dining room window. He was trimming off some of the branches with a small handsaw when, to my horror, he fell fifteen feet and landed on his back with a terrible thud. I grabbed the phone, dialed 911, and rushed to his side. Martha couldn't handle the sight of her husband lying there, and she ran inside. I was angry with myself and felt responsible for his injuries. He was gasping for air. I reassured him, just like the 911 operator had instructed. He had a look of what appeared to be pure devastation on his face, and just then I heard the sirens.

"Hang on, Tom. They're coming. You'll be fine. Do you hear them, Tom?"

By then, his eyes had glossed over. His body suddenly went limp. I knew in my heart he had died just then. The firemen were now by his side, working hard to save him, but it was no use.

All I could think about was what he'd said to me that morning: "I feel so good today. If this keeps up, I think I'll live to a hundred and ten."

I couldn't believe how fragile life could be. There were so many things I could have done, but nothing could change that now. There was something really odd about how disconnected I felt from the whole ordeal, as though my emotions were locked up. I went through the motions and took Martha with me to the hospital. She had no one, and their children lived out of the country. She knew he was gone, but I had a glimmer of hope that maybe they'd be able to revive him on the way. After all, Tom was a true fighter. I supported and comforted Martha when the doctor delivered the inevitable news that he didn't make it. She looked so fragile and broken. Her soul mate was gone, and it was apparent then that he took a part of her with him. It only hit me a few days later—hard, like a delayed reaction. It was as though it just happened. It took time to get the events of that day out of my mind, but the two of them will forever hold a special place in my heart.

We ran a small construction company out of our home. Work was inconsistent in the small city we lived in, and it seemed everybody was starting a business in order to create jobs. I left my job at the flooring company to work for a furniture store. The hours were much better, and I didn't have to make house calls. Five years at one place was a record for me, and I often wondered how people could stay somewhere so long. For some mysterious reason, I always seemed to get burned out after the first or second year of employment. Nevertheless, I was still working full-time and occasionally helped Julian with the paperwork. The economy was steadily getting worse. Even my sales suffered, and we were sinking more and more in debt. Something had to give soon. I felt like we were stuck in a funnel and there was nothing we could do to climb out.

I was feeling burned-out and saw my doctor for fatigue. He was very fond of Josh, and he saw us regularly. I don't know if he recognized something about our similarities, but he suggested Asperger's was believed to be genetic and wanted to refer me to a psychiatrist. I was shocked and refused the notion. As far as I was concerned, I was just burned-out. I stubbornly dismissed the idea and expressed my concerns about the stigma attached to such labels. He agreed. He went on to describe chemical reactions and how an imbalance can affect us. He said a chemical disorder is a physical condition, not a psychological one, and that it was nothing to be ashamed of. He then asked me what I would say if he could prescribe a medication that would give me my life back, like when I was young. That got my attention, but I was still reluctant to believe him. I refused to see a psychiatrist but agreed to try the medication.

He diagnosed me with a chemical imbalance and prescribed a serotonin reuptake inhibitor. In about a week, I finally felt like I had my life back. It's a mystery how I managed without medicine for all those years. I finally saw my life with a clarity I had never experienced before. I was free of anxiety, and I had an abundance of energy. It gave me more confidence, and I was more of a pleasure to be around.

It was as though someone turned on a light. I saw my world in a brand-new way. My mood had improved, and I was able to make sense of the things I'd done in the past. Julian supported me, and the relief on his face said it all. I felt peaceful and strong and vowed to live life to the fullest. I encourage and strongly recommend anyone with AS to explore the possibility of a serotonin reuptake inhibitor, since AS fits into the category of a chemical imbalance. I don't claim that this is a miracle drug; there are still many challenges for me to overcome. The medication helped me tremendously. I don't want to even imagine what my life would be like without it again.

> The anger and frustration was replaced with regret for all the pain I'd put my family through. I worked on trying to gain their trust and forgiveness.

Sara was working and living on her own. She ran away during the difficult times we'd had and went to live in a youth home. We were able to get family counseling, which did her a lot of good. In the sessions, the counselor suggested I get some one-on-one therapy and I stubbornly refused, thinking it was my daughter who needed it, not me. We eventually were able to find some common ground. The more time I was on my medication, the more I realized that her actions in our relationship were really reactions to how I treated her with my suspicious behavior. It took me a long time, but once I realized the whole picture, I was appalled at myself and at what I'd done to my child. I tried to explain things to her the best way I could. I asked for her forgiveness, all the while I wondered how I was going to forgive myself.

Sara worked at a retail clothing outlet, and her sales skills amazed me. I visited her once in a while and marveled at seeing her in action. She made me proud, and we started doing more together. Eventually, she took me shopping for a new wardrobe and she was proudly introducing me to her friends as her young mom. We were finally closer to where we wanted to be in our relationship, the new wardrobe she helped me pick out signified a new start for us as mother and daughter. I was surprised at how easily she forgave me. It took a while to gain her trust. However, our relationship has since been what it should be: nurturing. We love each other unconditionally, and although I can't take back all those years, I vowed to make things right if it was the last thing I did.

Things at work were interesting. They were running a contest for the most furniture sold. Each seat we sold awarded us points for our dartboard competition; every six points gave us a dart. The board hung on the showroom wall against an area rug, and everyone was gathered around. I was winding up for my first shot, doing my best to psych myself into getting it on the board. Anybody who knows me can tell you how uncoordinated I am. I felt the dart slip from my fingers. I released it a bit too late. The dart traveled forty-five degrees to the left and stuck in the wall between the legs of Roger, one of the owners. The room roared with laughter as they backed away to let me finish the other three darts. They found me hilarious, and I actually felt more comfortable around them than I did at any other job. By the way, this was a different furniture store. The first one I worked at slowly lost business, and I had to look out for myself. They seemed to welcome my eccentricities with their easygoing natures.

# Chapter 23

# Emotions and Intimacy

About a year passed, when my obsession with religion had diminished considerably. It was much less intense, but it still consumed my thoughts every now and then. The new medication I was on helped, and so did the therapy, but I was still unable to completely relax. Julian was patient through it all. The more he tried to reach me, the more I resisted, and it eventually drove him crazy. Although he took things slowly with me, I felt pressured and I could see his frustration.

If I wasn't cold, I was hot. There was no in-between. I didn't mean to make him feel excluded; it just happened that way, and my interests consumed my time. This sort of thing occurred for much of my adult life. This back-and-forth both surprised and confused Julian. He never knew how to approach me from one day to the next. I didn't have the words to explain it to him. He looked at me as if I was a totally different person. This was the person he adored with all his heart, his Gypsy girl. Julian couldn't understand my changing moods. He knew one side of me, which was wild, and the other side, which was reserved, and the inconsistency drove him crazy. It seemed I wore a different face every three to six months. I was enthusiastic and unpredictable for weeks on end. As soon as I became obsessed with my interests, I was preoccupied and he was lonely.

Half a year had passed without change, and Julian announced he was leaving me. It was the end of November. He said that I didn't feel real to him and he couldn't take it anymore. He thought this was the real me and said I wasn't the same woman. I didn't know who I was anymore, either; questions surrounding my identity still plagued me.

I lashed out at him, insisting he was heartless for throwing away the years we shared.

"How can you hurt our kids like that after all they've been through?"

He paced the floor, stopped, and said, "I can't stand it anymore. I never know who I'm going to come home to at the end of the day. One month you're confident and happy. The next month, you're insecure, depressed, and obsessed with religion or whatever else you happen to be into."

He sat next to me and calmly explained, "You're cold. You don't want to be touched. I don't get it, and I don't want to do this anymore. I'm tired, all right?"

I sat there trying to absorb what this incredible man was telling me. My thoughts were racing, and something inside of me went off. "That's fine. You can go ahead and throw it all away, but you're not going to hurt Josh in the process. I won't let you. Do you hear me? I don't want him to have to deal with any more than he has to. This is going to kill him. Don't you see that?"

"No, Babe. He'll be fine. It's a lot better than watching us argue all the time. You don't have to worry; we'll live together until after Christmas, and then I'll find a place to live. I'll take care of you and the kids, and I'll visit with them during the week and on weekends. I can't live with you anymore. I need you to let me get on with my life, please."

I could barely make out his face as I looked up at him through a blur of tears. "Tell me this then, Julian, and be honest with me. Do you have any love for me anymore?"

He looked at me and then looked away. "There's nothing left for me to give. The love is gone. I'm sorry!"

The devastation was more than I could take. This was actually happening, and there was nothing I could do to change it. I could beg him to stay, but his mind was made up. I broke down into a heap of agony and tears. We kept it from the kids and agreed to sleep in different beds until he found his own place after Christmas. Surprisingly, I managed to go to work. Mind you, I went through the motions of everyday life with a smile, but my insides were a living hell. With all the struggles we faced, I couldn't believe he stopped loving me.

I decided he must be confused and gave him his space in the hopes that he would come around. Several weeks went by. He assured me he would look after me until I got back on my feet. I feared then it was really over. There were many times in our lives when we argued and said we were ending it, but it didn't feel the same way this time. There was a finality to his words, and he was despondent. I went on about my days, pretending everything was fine for the kids' sakes.

Josh walked in from school with a look of satisfaction on his face. "Mom, there's only a few days left until school's out."

"That's great, Hon! Do you have any plans for your holidays?"

"I'm just going to relax. Probably play my computer games or something."

"Do you know what you want for Christmas?"

"I don't know, Mom. Maybe a Nintendo game."

He named off several games we'd rented recently, and I later wrote them down in my notepad. We had plans the following night to do some Christmas shopping. He was easy to buy for; his interests were quite narrow and he didn't care for anything else. I played Christmas carols and called Sara over to help us decorate the tree. I put on a bright smile, sang with all my heart, and we decorated our tree. It was beautiful, although to me it had a dull, empty look to it. I felt empty and sad.

Each day brought me closer to the inevitable loneliness I was going to have to endure.

I had never once talked to anyone about any problems in our relationship. I was nervous about crossing that line and didn't quite know how to tell them, so I just blurted it out and started to cry. I couldn't stop crying; the harder I tried, the more out of control I felt. They were taken aback and asked my why. I had trouble telling them. All I could say was what he told me, that we were too different and he didn't feel the same way about me anymore. Everyone who knew us saw us as inseparable, but they never really saw what our private lives were like. I kept it well-hidden. We were the last couple expected to separate. It wasn't long until his family was calling him and telling him he was crazy for leaving me.

> Christmas was for the children; I wasn't about to let it be ruined. I had to do everything I could to protect them. I knew above all else I had to remain strong. In a final, desperate attempt to keep him, I confided in Julian's parents about what was going on, which I'd never done before.

For as long as we could remember, others had referred to me as the perfect girlfriend, wife, mother, daughter, and employee. To everyone's surprise, Julian responded that he felt I was too perfect and no one understood him, but I knew that I did. The energy I put into keeping my real self hidden was exhausting. I tried so hard to please everyone. All my efforts were for nothing. Worse, they were the very reason our marriage was falling apart.

I'm not quite sure how or why, but something about repeating it to someone else finally made me realize what I had been doing and how it must have appeared in Julian's eyes. Why on earth was I so insistent on living like an android? I didn't know why, but I knew I was going to do everything I could to save our marriage. I had to let go of my fears and learn to relax.

Living all those years as someone else was going to be hard to unlearn, and I knew time was not on my side. I decided that night to come clean with Julian and hope for the best. I went to my tae kwon do class and had to leave early. I was so nervous about talking to him I had a full-blown anxiety attack. I managed to get to the car and drive home. I didn't want

Julian to see me out of control. It wasn't the best strategy for keeping your man, in my opinion. I walked in the side door, still shaking and hyperventilating, and tried to go to my room unnoticed. Julian saw me and asked me what was wrong. I told him I was all right, but one look at me and he quickly fetched me some water and a damp cloth. As my breathing subsided, I began telling him how I realized I was living a lie. He quietly watched me as I continued.

"I don't know why, but I always held back the parts of myself I didn't like. I was trying to mold myself into the ideal woman. I've been cheating myself and everyone else, including you, and for that I am so sorry, my love! I don't know why I've been doing that, but I realize it now, and I want to be myself."

He had tears in his eyes. He took me into his arms and what he said next took my breath away. "Babe, I love you. You're my yin, and I'm your yang. Do you know what yin and yang are? They're two parts that fit together perfectly. One part is white and the other is black, and they form a circle. We're complete opposites. I'm dark and you're light. We fit together perfectly and complete an eternal circle. You complete me; without my yin, I could never survive. I've never felt as lost as I have in this past month."

We held each other and cried, and he promised to never let me go.

I couldn't believe how things could change so much just by releasing my inhibitions. That day was the beginning of a new life with the real me, and I knew I had to be patient with myself.

Christmas was only a week away, and it was a wonderful time. We were both thankful to be together. The week flew by and we were like newlyweds rediscovering each other and enjoying our little family. The threat of losing everything such a short time ago showed us how to appreciate each moment we had, and Christmas that year was simply magical.

# Chapter 24

## Life-changing Move

The winter of 2001 was a long one and construction was slow, yet our bond only grew stronger as all the layers I had accumulated gradually peeled away. We talked about moving to Toronto. The economy in our city was horrible, and we were sinking deeper in debt. This was the push we needed. We started to prepare Josh and Sara for the possibility of moving. We both began our search for work in Toronto. This became my new quest, and within three months I accepted a position in a furniture store. During the interview, I told them I wasn't too crazy about going back to working weekends and evenings. The manager talked me into it, even though he knew I would be with them two years tops. It was difficult to find good employees in that area, and they seemed more excited about hiring me than I was about being hired. It felt quite nice to be appreciated for all the hard work I had poured into my career. My job was to start the following week. It was up to me to find an apartment while Julian looked after renting out the house and moving. Sometimes I thought I was crazy to be moving to a huge city far away from any extended family, but my determination was more powerful than the fear that tugged at me.

I drove around the city that Saturday morning in search of a room. I found a few possibilities through the want ads. There were places where I didn't even get out of the car, and I spent a lot of time trying to find my way around. It was frustrating. Most of the neighborhoods were so appalling I kept driving. For my last appointment, I pulled into a driveway of a little bungalow, fortunately in a decent neighborhood and only fifteen minutes from work. The landlord ran a business out of his home and rented the rooms. I took a room, but I found out later that the other tenants were all men and my landlord didn't even live there. That made me all the more nervous. I kept my door locked at all times and stayed in my room except when I went to work, got groceries, or went apartment hunting. The day I moved in and unloaded my belongings, I went through a series of irrational motions so that I could feel secure in this huge city. I started out by unlocking my bedroom door and bringing my things inside. Then I locked my bedroom door and went off to the locked car again for another load. I locked the car again, carried in more things, unlocked the bedroom door, and so on. I repeated this at least ten times until I was completely moved in.

Everyone commented on how brave I was. This validated my efforts and encouraged me to muster the courage to continue.

Other people questioned my motives. I heard ridiculous rumors that I was having an affair with one of the representatives at work and was leaving Julian to move in with him. This would have been extremely odd and out of character for me.

Once I put my mind to something, it usually becomes an obsession and I'm driven to make things happen. Within a month, we rented a beautiful condo on the city's outskirts. Julian had a high-paying job, and for the first time in ages we were on our way to a better life. I figured that by the time we settled in, we would be back on our feet within a year or two in the most.

I liked my new job, but the training I received there was limited. I called the representatives of each furniture line and arranged to meet with them so I could learn about their products firsthand. I always seemed to retain information best when I heard it firsthand.

I found the leather tanning process fascinating. The representative pointed out how the characteristics and markings on the hide told a story. He described how you could see the history of the hide by looking into the grain. He pointed out the many features of the hide's authenticity with hints of barbed wire scars and insect bites, as well as the soft and luxurious feel of top-quality leather. I quickly absorbed the information and became somewhat of an expert on the leather tanning process and furniture construction. I eagerly shared my knowledge with my customers so they could appreciate it through my eyes. I treated them with integrity and respect.

Within a few months, I ranked in the top three in sales, which made me happy, but my competitive nature was and still is almost non-existent. I was just interested in being prepared, doing my best, and enjoying myself in the process. Keeping busy was paramount for me, and I got involved in the decorating aspect with customers.

Lucas, the owner, had me help with the store's layout and design. He was impressed with my ability to visualize the finished product. He had his wife and mother come in to see the store and pick out one of the many floral arrangements I created for one of their dinner parties. Keeping busy was a great way to avoid the down time, when I was expected to interact with my co-workers. If I wasn't creating displays, I helped track the flow of customers to ensure everyone was looked after. I often dealt with three or four customers at a time. As long as it was directly related to a field I knew, helping customers wasn't so difficult, but I often wondered why they weren't able to picture the room setting I was trying to make them visualize.

The most challenging aspect of my job was remembering faces and people's names. This was nothing new. I'm what you would consider face blind, and I can forget a person's name immediately after hearing it, which can prove to be quite embarrassing. In one specific instance when I first started there, a customer asked for Lucas and I went looking for him. I walked right up to him and asked him if he saw Lucas; a customer was asking for him. He gave me a look of incredulous disbelief and said, "I'm Lucas. Remember? The guy who hired you?"

I often felt uncertain about approaching a customer for fear that I would greet the same person I'd already spoken with five minutes ago. This happened quite frequently.

Finding ways to remember customers by association was the only way I could come close to overcoming my problem. If that failed, I would watch the customer's facial expressions for clues of recognition and hope for the best.

Even after five years of working in sales, the most awkward part of my job was the small talk after the greeting. I would have found it much easier just to qualify their needs and supply them with the information they needed to make an informed and logical decision. I did, however, manage to develop a great way of getting over that initial fear of the greeting. I say "fear" because I would get a knot in my stomach when a customer entered the store. But I always wore a smile on my face to approach the customer. The method I used worked extremely well.

By using my imagination, acting skills, and the power of suggestion, I imagined the person was a relative. If a woman reminded me of an aunt, cousin, or sister, for example, I actually pretended she was that person. This was the very best way for me to deal with this issue. I felt more relaxed, and customers immediately felt connected to me, although they didn't quite understand why.

Almost every day, one of my customers would turn to their spouse and ask, "Who does Sophia remind you of?" They would name off a few people until they came to the conclusion that maybe I reminded them of their friend, sister-in-law, or niece. This fascinated me because they almost always got it right, considering my specific role at that time. One couple reminded me of people I babysat for as a teenager, and I immediately felt a warm connection with them. After helping them furnish their room, they told me they had been to the store down the street and found a better deal but came back to me because they trusted me. Customers rarely asked me for a better price. Before they left, I shook their hands as I always did, and they each gave me a warm hug.

This happened more frequently than I would have wanted. I really couldn't understand why people reached out to me like they did; it was quite embarrassing. An older couple came in one day. The woman reminded me of my mother in a small way, so I logically assumed the role of a daughter with her. Close to the end of their visit, she held my hand tenderly and told me I reminded her of her daughter. She wasn't letting go of me. Her husband gave me a helpless look and said they lost their daughter in a car accident a few years back. I felt terrible and astonished at the same time. Purely by accident, I found myself in the awkward position of giving someone the rare gift of feeling their daughter again. Before they left, I commented on how quickly the week went.

They laughed and said, "You got that right, Sophia! Wait till you get to our age. The older you get, the faster time flies."

I walked them out to their car and found myself saying, "You didn't lose her, you know, and it will never be 'good-bye,' but only 'so long.' Maria just got a head start. And besides, time flies, doesn't it?"

They smiled as they held each other. I never assumed the role of a daughter again. Even though I know I brought them comfort, I sensed their pain, which was too personal for me.

My boss marveled at the way customers related to me and asked me how I did it. Telling him the truth would only indicate to him that I was losing it, so I replied, "I'm not quite sure, exactly. I treat them like the individuals they are, not like customers, and everything else falls into place."

He kept trying to figure me out. He watched me closely. Sometimes he fluffed pillows nearby in the hopes of hearing my "spiel," as he called it. His father, Stan, the owner of the store, came in every day. He was in his mid-seventies. He was a sweet man, but even he would hide to try to listen to me. I caught him several times watching me from behind a fichus tree. He was actually in plain sight, which was comical. He talked to me every chance he got, and we ended up being good friends. My method of madness had become second nature to me, and I took the role of granddaughter with him. He told me stories of the struggles he experienced as a young man when he began his company. I respect that man to no end. He's real, and I think a lot of that comes with age. It was a shame that this job required me to work evenings and weekends. I really could have seen myself staying there until I retired.

# Chapter 25

# Overwhelmed by Opportunity

I was delighted when I saw an ad for the job of my dreams for a cosmetic company as an outside sales representative. I immediately got to work on my résumé, perfecting it until I was satisfied. By the time I finished it, it was well past three thirty in the morning. I couldn't believe how quickly the time went. I hurriedly submitted it by e-mail and went to bed, careful not to wake Julian. He always got upset with me if I wasn't careful about getting the sleep I needed. Sleep deprivation was always a major trigger for seizures, and he didn't think I was careful enough. I had to work the next morning, but like many nights, I lay in bed with thoughts running through my mind as I raced against time to get some sleep. My mind was consumed with thoughts of a great future and the freedom this new job would mean. I was very tired, and I didn't sleep more than three hours that night. I dragged myself out of bed and went to work, and of course I ended up with a frustrating customer. It was their fifth time in, and they still couldn't decide on which chair they wanted. They had me running back and forth for prices and quotes on custom orders with various grades of leather. Feeling dizzy, I excused myself to the other showroom to sit down and try to relax. I knew if I wasn't careful, I'd have a seizure.

Shortly thereafter, the inevitable happened. I had a full grand mal seizure and awoke in the hospital with Sara at my side. Nobody was able to reach Julian because he was on a construction site. Sara reassured me that everything was all right and that Julian would soon be there. She insisted I get some sleep. The nurse was still waiting for the doctor to prescribe the medication I needed. Once again, she urged me to get some sleep in order to prevent another seizure.

I awoke to the doctor's voice asking me all the basic questions to test my cognitive reflexes. Then she asked me if I drove to work. When I replied that I did, she said she had to file a report with the ministry of transportation to have my driver's license revoked. I pleaded with her to reconsider. I explained I had been seizure-free for eight years and my other doctor had weaned me from my medication. I told her that on my medication the seizures were perfectly controlled. Besides, before seizures I felt an aura ten to fifteen minutes ahead of time.

It was no use. She flat out told me she was still reporting me, and that was it. My dreams of landing the cosmetic job were crushed. She held my future in her hands, and I was angry at her indifference. I felt an aura coming on, and that's all I remember.

This time it was life-threatening. I wasn't breathing, and my face and lips were blue. They had to insert a breathing tube to clear my airway until the seizure ended. Sara was traumatized by what she witnessed. She thought I was dying. She often cried if she even thought about or was reminded of what happened that day. Due to lack of oxygen, my memory was affected. I gradually regained most of it, but it took months.

Lucas told me to take as much time as I needed before returning to work. He said I had scared everyone, and he didn't want a replay.

The seizures caused temporary amnesia. I took the time I needed to review as much information as I needed in preparation for my return to work. I also did crosswords.

Six weeks had passed, and my return to work was a little shaky. My memory came back, but it was frustrating to have to ask for help on things that came so naturally to me before. It was a grueling process, and I was fortunate that the damage was reversible.

My driver's license was reissued to me within six months, and I was back to my old self again. Gradually, Lucas began to let me deal with his biggest clients and personal friends. He advised me to keep things to myself and to be careful not to upset the other sales people. Nevertheless, within a year and a half I was working with Lucas on a major project, spearheading a commercial furniture department. I was working fifty to sixty hours a week, and we both knew it could take a good six months to see any substantial results. I kept at it, plugging away, making solid contacts within the film industry and with hotel chains and golf courses. To Lucas's surprise, I succeeded in arranging somewhat of a partnership with a commercial furniture supplier. We could take our customers to their showroom and share in the profits of these sales. This was perfect. Their showroom was just behind our store, and we didn't have to use up our space with extra inventory. It was so exciting. They provided me with training, and Lucas insisted I would be the only person granted access to their showroom. We made a lot of headway, but it was still a slow process. I kept working with my regular clientele due to the fact that my salary was small and the commission wasn't at a profitable margin yet. Some of the sales staff suspected I was getting a hefty salary and quickly grew resentful of me.

Little did they know that all the hard work I was putting into the company was due to my obsession with work. I wasn't asking for much in return. All I wanted was the commission on the sales I made and to be reimbursed for my gas.

# Chapter 26

## Daughter's Newfound Love

I was glad to have Sara home with us again. A year had passed since we moved to Toronto. Her presence filled the void that was left in our lives when she moved away. She loved Toronto but missed her friends back home. However, it was quite amazing to me how easily she made friends only a month after moving into a new city. She worked in a nightclub as a waitress and dated many guys, but quickly lost interest in them. One day she asked me if she could invite her new boyfriend to meet us. His name was Adam, and she got excited when she talked about him.

"He's so different, Mom. He's sweet, and all we do when we look at each other is smile. Come to think of it, I can't stop giggling when I'm around him. I think I'm in love, Mom!"

I'd never seen her so excited about anyone before. It was really sweet. "Who is he?"

"I met him at work. He's Chinese, and he doesn't speak any English."

"How do you understand each other?"

"We use hand signals or hold each other and kiss, and we teach each other just what we need to know. Oh, Mom, he's so cute and innocent, you'll fall in love with him, too."

We met Adam later that night, and she was right. He was sweet, had a genuine smile, and spoke little if any English.

He shook my hand and said, "How are you?"

"I'm good, Adam. How are you?"

"Good!"

"Sara tells me you met at her work."

"Yes, at her work."

I didn't know what else to say, so I said, "She's lucky to work there, because she met you."

His eyes suddenly lit up with a look of recognition. He understood something in what I said and replied, "No, Sara no lucky, I lucky," and he took her hand in his.

Their relationship flourished into something special. They made an adorable couple. Adam was a sweet young man who doted on her. He taught her Cantonese and she taught him English. Sara was in love, and eventually she was living a beautiful life with her fiancé, Adam. She had grown into a magnificent young woman and was modeling part-time for several agencies. It made me proud to see that, in spite of everything, she retained the values we instilled in her. They were a beautiful distraction for me, and I enjoyed them.

It was almost a year into their relationship when Sara announced she was pregnant. At first I was shocked and upset, but when she told me that they were happy about it, I was filled with emotions I didn't quite recognize. Then I realized we were going to have a baby. Julian and I were going to have a grandchild, and we were excited. How lucky could we be? It was like we were expecting our own child, and just the thought of watching our daughter enter this remarkable new phase excited us. I was telling everybody the good news, and it was wonderful to share in her pregnancy. Julian was glad, but he worried about the possibility of having to support them should things not work out between Sara and Adam. They struggled due to their cultural differences, only to grow closer to each other with each passing moment.

The guys I worked with were great. They saw me as their little sister and were clearly happy for me; they teased me about my new status and called me "sexy grandma." Thirty-nine was young to have a grandchild, and I always looked much younger than my age. People were always shocked to hear I was in my thirties, let alone my late thirties.

Nyles had been with the furniture store for over eighteen years and had recently been promoted to sales manager. He was a nice guy at first sight, but he had quite the jealous streak and often gave the other guys a hard time. He had a nasty way of playing one employee against the other. He got excited if it escalated into an argument, like it was his source of entertainment at work. He couldn't hide his frustration with my promotion and hated to see anyone happy. He started in on me, jumping at any chance to use his management position against me.

The last straw was when I returned from my weeklong holiday, only to be reprimanded by Lucas. Nyles told Lucas that I never notified him I was going on holiday. He said he had to scramble at the last minute to arrange for coverage, which was an outright lie. I booked my holiday with him two weeks prior. I talked openly about my plans for an entire week beforehand, and then reminded him on my last shift. I told Lucas that, and showed him where I booked it off on the staff calendar in our lunchroom. Nyles argued that I must have penciled it in after my return in order to save myself the embarrassment of forgetting to tell him. He then gently referred to the fact that I was forgetful due to the seizure I'd had. Perhaps that it could explain this whole situation.

I was speechless; I couldn't believe what he was insinuating. Lucas wasn't sure whom to believe. He actually asked me if it was possible that I forgot to tell Nyles and I just thought I had. You can only imagine how upset I was. After all, I put my heart and soul into this company, only to get a slap in the face upon my return from a well-deserved holiday.

I stood my ground. I told him what I thought of Nyles and his manipulative ways, and that there was no way I was going to take this from him or anyone else. It wasn't worth the trouble, and I knew it was time to move on.

I started my search for another job and told Lucas about my plans. He pleaded with me to stay, but I didn't have the energy to endure the likes of Nyles. Life was too short, and I wanted to free up my evenings and weekends for my family.

Josh needed me more now that he was an adolescent. I worried about him. He'd started showing signs of depression, and I needed to be available to him. I knew he was having difficulty fitting in at school; he was withdrawn and seemed quite unhappy these days. It was time to get a job where I had weekends and evenings off.

Within a few weeks I had another job. The staff was sorry to see me go, and they gave Nyles the cold shoulder. I began working for a company selling cemetery plots and prearrangements. I reasoned that the money was great and it gave me evenings and weekends off with my family.

It was a huge mistake on my part. I found the job to be too morbid for me. Shortly thereafter, I took a job in a call center. My evenings and weekends were free, and even if the money wasn't as good, the job was better for me and there were more chances for advancement. I thought the job suited me because I didn't have to make face-to-face contact with customers and small talk was minimal. The owner of this company was an old guy; he ran his company like a well-oiled machine, with emphasis on reward systems and employee satisfaction. This made for a happy and productive work environment. The team I worked on was nice, but I basically kept to myself. One of the girls asked me if they did something to offend me, which I found really surprising.

I simply responded that I was shy and it would take me a little while to get comfortable. Looking back at the situation, I realize how it must have seemed to them. I was outgoing with customers on the phone, due to my well-rehearsed acting skills, but I ignored my co-workers by trying to stay busy.

I found the job uncomfortable. It was a larger company with over three hundred employees, and I felt like I was in school again. It took me at least five months before I could really be myself. I eventually did make a few good friends. Jill was a kind woman with a great sense of humor and an infectious laugh. She was quite the comedian, and she made me laugh constantly when we were together. Noreen was exciting and had somewhat of a dramatic flair. She was from Africa, and her accent intrigued me. Carolyn was a delicate woman and a single mother of five. For some reason, I felt the need to take care of her. We always seemed to be laughing when we were together.

When stress is a real factor, the mood lasts longer and I start feeling depressed, but it doesn't go beyond more than a few days. I look for a means of escape by reading or getting involved in projects. Fortunately, it's never been very difficult to keep myself occupied.

There were days when I wished everything would stand still so I could get a break. It seemed to be some sort of mood swing, or maybe something more than that. It still happens sometimes. It's like a temporary feeling of utter hopelessness. I feel I can't go on, and wish I didn't have to work or look after any responsibilities. I'm not sure if it comes from exhaustion, or if it's my frame of mind, but it happens a few times a month and passes within a day.

# Chapter 27

# It's a Granddaughter

We bought a beautiful new home in the fall of 2004—on the exact same day Sara started her labor pains. It was an exciting day, to say the least. By the time her pains were two minutes apart, we met her at the hospital. I was impressed with Sara. She was exceptional throughout the entire ordeal. She even insisted we get some sleep because she wanted us to be wide awake by the time the baby came. Adam sat in his chair, unable to get any rest. He played video games on his laptop while I rolled up my jacket and tried to get some sleep. I couldn't help glancing over at Sara from time to time. She sat patiently through her pains until they became too much to bear. At 7:35 the next morning we were blessed with the birth of our sweet little granddaughter, Isabelle. She was absolutely adorable.

Witnessing my first-born child having her baby was indescribable. Adam was beside Sara, and I stood between Adam and the doctor, coaching and encouraging her.

Julian was just outside the partially open door, so he heard everything, including Isabelle's first cry. As soon as she was born, we invited Julian in to meet her. He was crying like he did when our own babies were born. She looked like Adam, with a touch of Sara's features. She stared at each of us, as though to memorize our faces. I watched them bond with their new baby; I couldn't believe time had gone so fast. It didn't seem so long ago that Julian and I were bonding with Sara.

Suddenly I felt like they should be alone to create their own memories. We kissed the baby and the new parents and left. We drove home that morning exhausted and satisfied, eagerly awaiting our next visit. We called everyone we could think of with the news, and I took pictures into work to show my co-workers our beautiful granddaughter.

The move to the new house was uneventful, except that we lost a box of files: receipts and backup files we had for our business. We even lost our computer files due to a virus. To make a long story short, we were audited and stiffed with a huge tax bill. Each payment we made brought me closer to yet another obsession. I pulled out every receipt I could, dating back seven years, so we could backtrack on things we hadn't claimed before. Sorting all my receipts in a chronological sequence took me over two months. I took out six library books to learn everything I could about tax loopholes, and my days were consumed with recording everything to the penny. In the end, we saved over fifteen hundred dollars, which was well worth the time it took to do it. Besides, knowing our finances were in order was comforting. I incessantly shared my newfound knowledge with anyone who would listen, and I encouraged them to do the same.

# Chapter 28

# The Moment of Truth

One Tuesday morning later that fall, the president of the call center announced his official retirement. His son Craig would take his place as head of the company. Craig was charming and suave. He reminded me of a politician, and he didn't waste any time announcing huge changes. He reached many of us with his motivational speech, and the room was a buzz of excitement. Within a short time, it was apparent that the changes he made were impacting the employees in a negative way. The once happy, productive company was transformed into a virtual sweatshop in as little as three months. Before too long, they lost their share of hard-working, ethical employees. I decided to hold on for another six months to see if things would improve, but they got progressively worse.

With the new changes in place, it became increasingly difficult to work. I had a quota to call at least a hundred and fifty customers each day, send out samples and e-mails, and handle all the necessary administrative duties—it was like a race against time, and I was losing. The supervisors walked up and down the aisles urging us to sell enough to make budget by noon. It was sad. We were all in constant danger of losing our jobs, and tension was high. I sometimes found that working under pressure could be stimulating, but with the new changes and the severe method of micro-management, it was difficult to manage my stress level.

I sort of felt sorry for the managers. The tension in the call center was unbelievable, and even their positions were in jeopardy. This job was draining me. Most days I got home, had dinner, and went straight to bed.

I couldn't seem to stay awake. There was a quiet room at work, and I often took to it in exhaustion to sleep during lunch or break. It was absolutely dreadful; the stress was getting to be unbearable.

My supervisor, Cathy, took notice. One day, in front of everyone, she asked me flat-out if I was autistic.

I replied, "No! Why would you ask me that?"

She pointed to my hands and, to my horror, I realized why. My fingers and thumbs were going a mile a minute. I'd always had control of my ticks in public; it was upsetting to see what this place was doing to me. I said, "It's just stress. My son has AS, and I may have some features, but that's about it."

She said she noticed me doing it almost every day. I tried to laugh it off and said, "See what this place does to you?" I felt scrutinized and vulnerable, and I knew I had to get out of that environment.

I have to say, even though I didn't appreciate the way she approached me, I'm thankful to have met her. Otherwise I might still be in denial. She was an intelligent woman, but quick to speak without thinking. Her honesty forced me to examine my life. As time went by, I tried to notice the features I was displaying. As I added them all up, it was undeniable.

Still unsure, I asked Julian what he thought. He said he'd suspected I had AS for years now. He kept it to himself before because he didn't want to upset me and didn't feel I was ready to hear it. He was right, but I was disappointed that he didn't trust me enough to talk to me before. He explained I had all the features that Josh had, and he suggested some of my family members did, as well. That would explain why it took me so long to make any type of connection. He pointed out our odd sense of humor, our shyness, and our loss for words in conversation. It also explained our gentle demeanors, long-term memory retention, and unexplained obsessions.

From that day onward, I tried to see myself in a more objective way. I started to really see how my habits seemed to relate to the characteristics associated with AS, and things made more sense to me.

Josh started to regress, and there were signs of depression due to an ongoing problem with kids at school. His principal called me away from work with a serious issue he'd been having. Josh was depressed and couldn't hide his pain anymore. He confessed to having thoughts of harming the kids who teased him. He was clearly upset and said he'd been feeling this way for over four years. I took him immediately to see a psychologist. After a few sessions, his anxieties diminished. But the pain still showed, and there was nothing I could do except comfort and reassure him.

The psychologist gave him the coping skills to turn his once-disturbing fantasies into a positive frame of mind. She suggested that he change the outcome of his thoughts by imagining he was reasoning with them until they backed off and apologized. This method of desensitization was what he needed to give him some control of his thoughts and emotions, and these episodes diminished over time.

It's quite interesting to see how things can be perceived when you only see the surface of someone with AS, versus what really goes on inside. To Josh, the recurring thoughts of harming his tormentors frightened him because his thoughts transferred into vivid actions, like those in movie clips. These repeated against his will, especially in times of stress. You can imagine that this would make anyone feel panicked. The outside perception might have been that his fantasies were a desperate fixation to exact vengeance on his pursuers. When he came to me with this, he was clearly upset, and he was relieved at finally confessing the secret he'd been dealing with all that time. He knew he would never have acted on those thoughts, but he knew it wasn't normal and was tremendously confused. Josh never wanted vengeance. It was literally his ability to think in pictures that haunted him all those years.

> The better he was able to control his troubling thoughts, the less often they occurred. Finally, they diminished altogether.

The ability to think in pictures amplifies everything, from actions to emotions. What some people consider a curse can also be considered a gift. If I think of it enough, I can feel like a child. It's a wonderful feeling, actually. You see everything through the eyes of yourself as a child. That's one of the great gifts of Asperger's. It's likely due to the fact that I think in pictures. They are so vivid and clear that the emotions come through as well. Someone with AS automatically assumes that everyone else sees the world in the same way. I myself only recently learned that the typical person's thought process is made up of mostly words, with limited actions or pictures.

This takes me back to a conversation I had with Josh where he demonstrated his ability to think in pictures. He suggested to me that in order to access energy effectively, man could probably use an intricate system of mirrors in space to reflect or deflect the sun's rays to or from specific regions. He said if the mirrors were built in panels, we could control the intensity and location of the energy reflected to earth or away from it. This would give us precise control and prevent global warming or another ice age, among many other things. He quickly drew a detailed blueprint from his mental image. He concluded that even though he thought it would work, in today's society, someone would undoubtedly use it for destructive purposes.

In certain instances, when this feature is amplified, you will find the likes of brilliant artists thought to have AS, like Michelangelo. Many artists are able to see what they are painting in intricate detail before their brush even touches the canvas. In the case of my son and I, this is only amplified to a certain degree. We lack the intricate details, seeing them only like an out-of-focus movie clip. The same goes for the other senses. Think of a gifted pianist who can play a piece after hearing it played once. It's engraved in his memory to retrieve and use as he wishes.

I believe echolalia, which is a tendency to repeat something out loud or in your mind, may play a huge role in retaining pieces of information so accurately. I say this because as children and to this day, Josh and I still repeat strings of sentences in our minds. This is particularly true if we enjoy the sound of what is being said, and it actually repeats in the same tone, like a recorder playing over and over. I can't really explain why for certain, but I do know that it feels satisfying to play it over.

> The best way to describe the satisfaction it brings is to say it feels like I'm making it my own, to use as I wish.

I believe this is what contributes to features Hans Asperger referred to as "the little professor." Most people with AS are known to have a sophisticated vocabulary. I have mentally collected many favorite songs and sayings over the years, even from my childhood. At times it can be enjoyable, but most often it's quite annoying. For some reason, at odd times, especially when I'm getting ready in the morning, a childhood lullaby plays over in my mind. If I'm in a hurry, the *Spiderman* theme song seems to be the song of choice. The thing that annoys me the most is when I can't prepare myself for the unpredictable. For my parents' thirtieth wedding anniversary, we reserved a section in a quaint little restaurant to celebrate with our friends and relatives. We had over fifty guests, and it was rather intimate. We sat at the head table with our parents, and the guests sat in rows facing our table. Everything was going great until it was time to say a few words, which had never even occurred to me. Natalie handed me the mike and whispered that I was elected emcee. I was unimpressed, to say the least. Then I stood there thinking, *I can do this. I'll just say a few words about them and thank everyone for being here.*

As I began, I realized that wouldn't be quite enough. My mind was racing through memories of good and bad times, and for some reason the times I'd watched them bicker stuck out in my mind. After congratulating my parents, I stood between them. For lack of knowing what else to say, I asked the crowd to join me in singing "Happy Anniversary." All eyes were on me as I started singing. The crowd of family and friends looked at me in confusion, and no one joined in. I was in the middle of the song when I realized I was singing the *Flintstones* theme song. My parents were blushing. We have it on video and, trust me: it's worse than it sounds. Then again, I can easily replay this embarrassing memory in my mind without the help of a video.

It's as though the initial memories that are formed in childhood are somehow connected through association, which in turn manifests itself into these thoughts. By beginning to understand the dynamics of echolalia, I firmly believe it can be possible to use it to our advantage. Might we someday succeed in unscrambling or controlling the complexities of how our minds store or filter information? The biggest drawback here is that if your interests are too narrow, the information you absorb tends to be limited. I'm sure this sounds really familiar to those of you with AS. It may sound a little strange to most people, but that's another small peek inside the mind of someone with AS.

This is a poem Josh wrote on the day his principal called me into his office. He was thirteen, and I was late in meeting up with them at school. It reveals the way he thinks and how he manages to cope with everyday frustrations in his own logical style.

### Time
*A thing that never stops,*
*never waits for anything;*
*It destroys things at a slow pace,*
*rusts, eats, kills, destroys;*
*We can't stop it, we can't control it,*
*yet we live with it every day;*
*We use time to our advantage,*
*in small doses it is harmless;*
*In large doses, it is a highly lethal weapon;*
*We can't run from it, we can't hide from it,*
*No one can escape it;*
*It will get me, it will get you,*
*it will get everyone;*
*So live life and enjoy life,*
*before time eats at you.*

It took Josh about five minutes to write this poem. He expresses his thoughts quite well in writing, but he very seldom expresses his emotions. Therefore, it took an abundance of time to finally understand and experience life through his eyes. I feel fortunate to be able to help my son by being able to see inside his world. My own experiences are, in essence, significant points of reference in helping Josh develop the skills and understanding he needs early in life.

My main goal is to spare him the trials and suffering that comes with AS. Most importantly, I want to help him use it to his advantage.

In my continued search for answers, I came upon an Internet forum for AS. As I browsed, I became aware of another woman on the site. I couldn't believe how much she reminded me of myself in terms of her thought process and the way she spoke. I couldn't help but marvel at how her style and even her personality resembled mine. It was as though I had written the text myself. I went through more forums, and they were all similar. Her style was simply uncanny. I should have answered her, but I didn't feel ready yet.

I came upon a Web site with an Aspie quiz and another site with a more formal diagnostic tool called the autism spectrum quotient. Both confirmed my suspicions. The first quiz showed that I was more Aspie than neuro-typical. Then I took a second quiz that was more in-depth. This was extremely accurate, in my opinion. I deliberately answered the questions as conservatively and honestly as possible. It was remarkable to me that the questions seemed like they were meant for me. I could relate to the majority of them. The results confirmed AS and gave me a score of thirty-seven out of fifty. A score of thirty-two and above met the criteria for high-functioning autism or Asperger's and, coupled with a certain level of distress, merited a referral for a full diagnostic assessment. Although a formal diagnosis can be intimidating, it can also serve to extinguish any lingering doubts about your struggles.

I am a very private person. Putting everything on paper has been a huge step for me, but it's a small price to pay if it means reaching those in need. Josh and I have grown closer these past couple of months. We have great discussions about both our interests and our likes and dislikes. We love to analyze situations and people and imagine what the future of the world will hold.

# Chapter 29

# Self-discovery and Emotional Healing

By 2006, I left my job due to stress and was hired as a customer service agent with a major postage equipment supply company, which turned out to be much less demanding. Since I began working there, I made a few friends and we sometimes have lunch together. But the majority of the time, I prefer to go out during lunch, or just read. I find myself still feeling shy and uncomfortable, even after a year. Over time, my position has proven to be quite challenging, but my skills have increased and I'm gradually getting used to it. There is so much information to remember that it can be overwhelming at times. That being said, my employer is very understanding, and for that I am grateful.

> I believe that forcing myself to use parts of my brain in ways I'm not accustomed to can only be beneficial in stimulating the areas that need it most.

I finally made the decision to see my family doctor so I could get a referral to a psychiatrist. It was a very uncomfortable experience since she was a new doctor and I'd only seen her a few times before. I told to her that my son was diagnosed with AS when he was a child. Although I was diagnosed with an anxiety disorder, I believed that I had AS and the anxiety was merely a symptom. When she asked me why I thought I had it as well, I said we were both alike. "I have as much difficulty with small talk as he does; in fact, I can't stand it. I'm uncomfortable in my own skin. I've always preferred my own solitude, and I have always had obsessive interests." I told her I needed to know so I could help my son. In order to do that, I needed to understand myself.

She referred me to a psychiatrist, and it was a long three weeks until I saw him. Getting ready for my ten o'clock appointment, I was shutting down my computer at work. Since I had to walk, I was glad the office was close to work. I was feeling guilty and stressed-out because, as usual, I'd waited until the day before to tell my manager about my appointment. Secondly, I never did confirm exactly where the doctor's office was. It never failed. Procrastinating, especially over personal appointments, was a normal occurrence. I walked out and realized I didn't know the address, only the major intersections, and realized I'd left my appointment book on my desk. By the time I ran back in and called the doctor's office for the address, it was nine-fifty. I was frantic. My appointment was at the local hospital, and it was at least a twenty-minute walk. This was ridiculous and frustrating. I rushed out, walked a quarter of the way, and managed to wave down a cab to get there in the nick of time.

Before I knew it, the psychiatrist was assessing me. An hour later, he went on to confirm I had strong Asperger traits: anxiety and paranoia. Could he have perceived the awkward self-consciousness I described to him as paranoia? I stared at him in astonishment and asked him how he could be so sure. He said he didn't specialize in treating people on this spectrum, but he treated a few people with autism. I gave him the quizzes I'd filled out, but instead of looking at them, he merely put them into the file. The interview, in my opinion, was incomplete. There were many things I couldn't think of then that I should have mentioned. I forgot to tell him about my intense hunger to learn and how forgetful I can be. I never mentioned my tendency to subconsciously curl my toes or shake my feet. There was just so much he didn't know about me. I certainly didn't expect to be diagnosed in one day. He explained how adults with Asperger's syndrome are difficult to diagnose because many symptoms can be masked by a lifetime of learned coping skills. He said he thought I might also be suffering from paranoia.

My thoughts were racing a mile a minute. Suddenly, Josh came to mind. All I could think about at that moment was Josh and his future, and I couldn't hold back the tears. A small part of me struggled with the thought that the doctor might be wrong; another part of me reasoned that he must know what he's talking about. He looked so sure of himself. However, I was a little put off by the fact that he didn't need to hear anything more. He started me on an antipsychotic medication and stressed the importance of proper treatment.

Finally, at forty-one, I was getting the help I needed to properly function. At that moment, I realized without a doubt that Josh would be fine. What a relief it was to know exactly what we were dealing with. Better yet, I now had the tools I needed to help our son and myself.

I found myself with an odd sense of serenity. After all those years, I was suddenly able to understand the many reasons for my actions. Nonetheless, I was filled with an overwhelming need to put my doubts to rest. I spent days reading up on all the topics I could find in terms of paranoia, and I didn't feel I fit the description. The doctor was right about many things, and I think he may have gotten my diagnosis pretty close. I have since been referred to a psychiatrist who specializes in autism spectrum disorders. There's a waiting list, but it appears that Josh and I will be seeing him soon. I would strongly recommend seeking a diagnosis for anyone suspecting autism or AS, no matter what age.

This book is my latest obsession. The fixations are becoming more and more productive now. I have to say, it's one of the strongest ones I've had in years. My mind races from the time I get up in the morning until the moment I fall asleep. Getting into anything else is a real challenge, and I have to stop myself from talking about it too much. Each morning I get up at six o'clock, head out to the coffee shop in the plaza where I work, sit at the exact same seat, and write until I start work at nine. I eagerly await the next fixation, obsession, or quest; hopefully, it'll be as fulfilling.

Julian and I celebrated our twenty-first wedding anniversary this year. This has been a phenomenal year for us. It feels like it's only been ten years tops, and we've been closer to each other than we have ever been before.

> The commitment I made to myself to completely open up to him about my inner, most private thoughts has given me a new perspective on life. It has shown me how trusting in the people I love can only result in a sense of acceptance and belonging.

Julian loves my world; he finds it interesting and eagerly joins me in anything I undertake.

My personal relationships with my parents, siblings, and immediate family have flourished to a level I never would have imagined before.

Today, I'm delighted to say that I've grown in so many ways because of this book.

Self-discovery has been the most rewarding experience of my life. However, I must say it's been emotionally draining. Julian's glad to be there for me. Sara can finally begin to understand why she endured the pain she went through, as well as the love and respect I have for her. Isabelle is growing into a miniature Sara. This child loves so much. If you were to walk her to the park, she'd take your hand and shower it with kisses of appreciation. I now have a chance to enjoy my Sara, through this child, the way I was meant to. Josh and I have bonded in a special way. We both understand and feel for each other. He claims that my AS is more prevalent than his, but in a cute way. I love his way. We have each other, and we understand each other fully.

There's something about what he told me the other day that validated all my efforts to reach him. He told me that he and his friend like to fool around in class while the teacher's back is turned. That statement would probably make most parents cringe, but to us, it was a promising achievement. He used to say that friends were too much of a commitment. He preferred his Internet buddies because they had more in common and stimulated his mind. I can already see some of the new social skills he's picked up. He especially has a soft spot for vulnerable people and reaches out to offer them comfort. In February, we were driving back home from visiting our family and stopped at a coffee shop when Josh did something that was completely out of character for him. There were two girls selling flowers outside in the freezing cold. He looked at them for a moment and said, "They look cold. Maybe we should get them a coffee." Surprised by his comment, we immediately gave him some change. He bought the coffee and took it to them.

I find it extremely important to respect Josh's space, and he appreciates that. We do struggle a little with the amount of time he spends in his room online. These days, he's into MMORPG, which stands for massive multi-player online role-playing games.

Role-playing games are known to be positive for people on the autism spectrum, for obvious reasons. Playing these games can help prepare people for real life scenarios. However, it's equally important to find a healthy balance. We usually accomplish this by encouraging Josh to spend more time with friends and family by planning weekend visits once in a while.

By doing that, we've noticed that he seeks our company more often now. He'll also take the dog for daily walks to the park. Julian says that, gradually, he will grow and his interests will change. Josh is growing up so fast. He told us just the other day that he was thinking about becoming a writer in his spare time to help get him through college. Julian and I are so proud of Josh. We can now see that he'll be fine and that he, too, will find his way.

We share more than just family traits; we share Asperger's. My greatest regret in life is not facing mine sooner. It would have made a huge difference in my son's life, not to mention my own. I've noticed that I'm more relaxed. Now I realize how uptight I could be at times. There's still a long way to go, but I now take comfort in knowing the direction I'm taking will only bring me closer to my goal. My conservative nature is starting to take a backseat, and in its place sits a more fun-loving soul.

> I've learned that laughter is a huge necessity for anyone with AS or autism-and everyone else, for that matter. It is a major ingredient in our lives now, and I must say that Josh and I have both learned to take life less seriously.

Before this book, we always assumed that everyone else's thought patterns were like ours. But after discovering the special way our brains are wired, I have to say we love ourselves more now for who we are. Using my firsthand experiences and learned coping skills have been my best tools. And so my quest continues.

# Conclusion

# Recommended Treatments

AS is more of a gift than a curse, and we would never want to have it completely taken away. Josh and I both appreciate the special abilities and gifts attached to the previously dreaded label of Asperger's syndrome now that we understand the unique abilities associated with it.

My personal definition of AS consists of these major traits:

- an individual who enjoys his or her solitude
- is shy and introverted but socially curious
- experiences difficulties with thought processing and expressive language
- can master impressive acting skills
- tends to persevere over varied yet limited interests
- has an intense hunger for knowledge
- has an unusual ability to think in images
- possesses phenomenal long-term but poor short-term memory
- has original thoughts and favors a systematic, logical thought process
- appreciates the benefits of routine and sameness
- tends to subconsciously self-stimulate
- has innocent and ethical qualities
- has a strong dedication to what he or she considers to be significant

If you suspect your child has Asperger's or autism, see your pediatrician for a referral to a professional who specializes in autism spectrum disorders. In the meantime, there are many good books out there, which are listed in the resources section of this book. These books were instrumental in my quest to develop coping skills geared to both my son's and my own situation. They offer tips to parents and professionals alike.

According to the National Institute of Neurological Disorders and Stroke National Institutes of Health Bethesda, MD 20892, the ideal treatment for AS coordinates therapies that address the three core symptoms of the disorder: poor communication skills, obsessive or repetitive routines, and physical clumsiness. There is no single best treatment package for all children with AS, but most professionals agree that the earlier the intervention, the better. An effective treatment program builds on the child's interests, offers a predictable schedule, teaches tasks as a series of simple steps, actively engages the child's attention in highly structured activities, and provides regular reinforcement of behavior.

This kind of program generally includes:

- social skills training, a form of group therapy that teaches children with AS the skills they need to interact more successfully with other children
- cognitive behavioral therapy, a type of "talk" therapy that can help the more explosive or anxious children to manage their emotions better and cut back on obsessive interests and repetitive routines
- medication, for co-existing conditions such as depression and anxiety
- occupational or physical therapy, for children with sensory integration problems or poor motor coordination
- specialized speech/language therapy, to help children who have trouble with the pragmatics of speech—the give and take of normal conversation
- parent training and support, to teach parents behavioral techniques to use at home

I love my mind and the thoughts that keep me entertained; I wouldn't want any of that to change. Otherwise, for me, life would no longer be interesting.

Isn't that what AS is all about? We strive to understand the true value of things, to see them for what they really are. We are collectors of facts. If there was one thing I wish we didn't have to deal with, it would have to be anxiety. That's a big one, and it's a significant part of our lives. Josh and I would be different people altogether had we been born without AS. I am confident that the difficulties we face each day will only get easier from this point on. If more emphasis could be placed on adults with AS or autism, in terms of services or studies, we could get that much closer to understanding the mysteries of AS and autism.

The ultimate goal would be to find a way to exclusively target and treat the negative aspects of AS. This alone would open up a realm of possibilities beyond any expectations imaginable. Some people on the spectrum feel that finding a cure could be detrimental, in the sense that it would most certainly alter one's personality and remove the positive aspects of this condition. In my opinion, the maturity and experience adults on this continuum can offer is priceless. That alone could get us that much closer to finding easier ways for people to cope with these challenges. After all, the autism-Asperger's continuum has a language of its own. I challenge anyone out there with these or other types of difficulties to step up. Voice your own experiences in order to bring us closer to finding the ultimate treatment. I am grateful to have been able to muster the courage to contribute in some small way by providing much-needed answers to the questions surrounding Asperger's and autism.

This book is my passion, my breath, and my voice. For me, there is no turning back. I have exposed my true self and, in the process, opened the doors to freedom, acceptance, and understanding.

This year, I have gradually begun to strip away tiny layers of what I call pretentiousness, only to uncover the girl inside. The girl who desperately needed to show the world who she really is inside, but who only now found the courage. The girl who tried to earn acceptance by being what she thought she should be instead of trusting who she really is. Through self-discovery and acceptance, I am able to give my son the wisdom of my experience and the encouragement he needs. Most importantly, I hope to have made an impact on the lives of many of you by providing the coping skills and understanding needed to achieve the proper balance many are so painfully denied. I wish you all the best in your quest to find your way through this mysterious yet fascinating syndrome called Asperger's, and I bid you all a fond farewell.

# Resources

## References

Ashley, Susan (2006) *The Asperger's Answer Book: The Top 300 Questions Parents Ask* Sourcebooks, Inc.

Baron-Cohen, S., Wheelwright, R.S., Martin, J., and Clubley, E. *"Journal of Autism and Developmental Disorders"* 31, 5-17 (2001) Publication, University of Cambridge, UK.

Grandin, Temple (1995) *Thinking In Pictures and Other Reports from My Life with Autism.* New York, NY: Doubleday.

Romanowski Bashe, P., Kirby, B.L., Attwood, T. (Foreword) (2005) *The OASIS Guide to Asperger Syndrome: Completely Revised and Updated: Advice, Support, Insight, and Inspiration,* New York, NY, Crown.

Stoddart, Kevin P., (2005) *Children, Youth and Adults with Asperger's Syndrome,* London, NI, Jessica Kingsley Publishers.

Hebb, D.O. Professor of Psychology at Carnegie Mellon, and Minshew, N., professor of psychiatry and neurology at the University of Pittsburgh School of Medicine and director of its Center for Autism Research. (2006) *"Scientists Discover Biological Basis for Autism",* Pittsburgh. Medical News Today.

## Web sites:

www.aspergersyndrome.org
www.asperger.org
www.tonyattwood.com.au/

www.aspennj.org
www.jpk.com
www.nas.org.uk
www.autismspeaks.org
www.firstsigns.org
www.nichd.nih.gov/autism
www.wmich.edu/aba/contents.html
www.nas.org.uk
www.autism-resources.com
www.autismwebsite.com/ari/index.htm

# About the Author

**Sophia Summers** is an adult with Asperger's Syndrome. She is an independent freelance writer, an active researcher, advocate of Autism Spectrum issues and a member of Autism Today. Formerly a sales and marketing executive for a furniture company, she currently works in a customer service department of a major corporation. Sophia lives in the Toronto area with her husband and son.

978-0-595-44932-3
0-595-44932-8

Lightning Source UK Ltd.
Milton Keynes UK
28 February 2011

168355UK00002B/239/A